Lutherans and Episcopalians Together

LUTHERANS AND EPISCOPALIANS TOGETHER

A Guide to Understanding

G. SCOTT CADY
CHRISTOPHER L. WEBBER

COWLEY PUBLICATIONS
Cambridge · Boston
Massachusetts

Published in the United States of America by Cowley
Publications, a division of the Society of St. John the Evangelist.
No portion of this book may be reproduced, stored in or introduced into a retrieval system, or transmitted, in any form or by
any means—including photocopying—without the prior written permission of Cowley Publications, except in the case of
brief quotations embedded in critical articles and reviews.

Library of Congress Cataloging-in-Publication Data:
Webber, Christopher.
    Lutherans and Episcopalians together : a guide to under-
standing / Christopher L. Webber, G. Scott Cady.
    p. cm
    Includes bibliographical references.
    ISBN 1-56101-191-6 (alk. paper)
    1. Evangelical Lutheran Church in America—Relations—
Episcopal Church. 2. Episcopal Church—Relations—
Evangelical Lutheran Church in America. 3. Anglican
Communion—Relations—Lutheran Church. 4. Lutheran
Church—Relations—Anglican Communion. 5. Christian
union—United States—History.   I. Cady, G. Scott, 1948–
II. Title.
BX5928.5.E95 W43 2001
280'.042—dc21   2001028051

Scripture quotations are taken from *The New Revised Standard
Version* of the Bible, © 1989, by the Division of Christian
Education of the National Council of the Churches of Christ in
the United States of America. Used by permission.

Cynthia Shattuck, editor; Vicki Black, copyeditor and designer
Cover design by Vicki Black

This book was printed by Data Reproductions in the United
States of America on recycled, acid-free paper.

Cowley Publications
28 Temple Place   •   Boston, Massachusetts 02111
800-225-1534   •   www.cowley.org

In appreciation of our partnership in ministry with St. Peter's Evangelical Lutheran Church and the Chapel of All Saints' in Cornwall

CONTENTS

PREFACE

Some years ago a Lutheran church and an Episcopal church were scheduled to take part in an ecumenical service at the Episcopal church to celebrate the week of prayer for Christian unity. That day the Lutheran pastor phoned the Episcopal priest.

"What color vestments should I wear?" asked the Lutheran. "Well," said the Episcopalian, "since this is the Season after the Epiphany, we would normally wear green."

"Oh!" said the Lutheran. "In Epiphany, we wear white." "But this is also St. Paul's feast day," the Episcopalian went on, "and on St. Paul's day we wear white."

"Yes," said the Lutheran, "but on St. Paul's day *we* wear red."

Since that time, Lutheran customs have changed and both ministers would now wear green in the season after the Epiphany. But the customs of that time revealed an underlying aspect of ecumenical relationships which is still true. The clergy in the story had a choice between observing the same day or season and wearing different colors, or wearing the same color in observance of a different day or season. In other words, if they looked alike, they would actually be celebrating different things, and if they looked different, they would be celebrating the same thing! Appearances can prevent us from seeing reality!

Relationships between Christians are sometimes like that. The divisions among us have a long history, and over the centuries we have adopted many different customs, beliefs, and practices in response to changing circumstances. Some of these differences have deep emotional meaning, while some are superficial; some appear divisive yet may conceal a deeper unity. Still others may reflect special insights and understandings that might benefit all Christians.

In the United States the Christian faith is lived out through a rich variety of church traditions. American Christians have often moved from one church to another, perhaps because there was no church of their denomination in a new community, or because they married someone of another background, or simply out of restlessness and a desire to grow in new ways. Most of us have spouses, cousins, ancestors, children, friends, or colleagues who go to different churches and with whom we sometimes discuss our churches and our differences. Sometimes those differences are painful, but often they give us insights into how much we have in common. Sometimes we even notice that a particular church of a different denomination is more familiar to us than another church of our own denomination. Such experiences lead many of us to ask how important our differences really are and how important it is to maintain them. Especially in recent years, churches in many communities have begun to work together on common projects and to worship together on special occasions. We have begun to understand how much we have in common and how much we can learn from one another.

For more than thirty years representatives from the Lutheran and Episcopal churches in the United States have met together to study what we have in common, what are our differences, and how we might come closer together. Through a series of votes in 1997, 1998, and 2000, both churches have adopted a specific proposal known as Called to Common Mission (CCM) to build a stronger and closer relationship. This new relationship may create a new way forward in ecumenical relationships, and it may be the most important step ever taken by Christians to overcome the divisions created by the Reformation. The decision was made by elected representatives of both churches, but now those of us who are members need to explore its meaning for ourselves, and how we can live it out in our individual churches and communities. This book is intended to help readers understand our two traditions and begin to explore the consequences of this new agreement. We invite you to use it in groups of both Lutherans and Episcopalians, but it can also be used in either church alone. Study materials for various kinds of groups of different ages interested in exploring further what this relationship can mean are available from LeaderResources (see the Resources for Further Study section at the back of the book for more information).

This book grew out of a joint Lenten program between our two congregations to help further understanding in the light of Called to Common Mission. Both of us have learned a great deal in writing this book, not only about the other church but also about our own. More important, we have gained a broader vision of the gospel and a deeper relationship with the one Lord who calls us into unity, ministry, and worship.

Members of the congregations we serve have read these pages and made many helpful suggestions. Our thanks to Joanne Wojtusiak, Sylvia Nielsen, and Henry Westmoreland for this assistance. The first two are Episcopalians and the third is a Lutheran—one more indication that when we approach each other without preconceptions we are often wonderfully surprised by what we find.

G. SCOTT CADY
CHRISTOPHER L. WEBBER

CHAPTER ONE

OUR COMMON HERITAGE

Lutherans and Episcopalians in History

On October 31, 1517, a monk named Martin Luther walked up to the front door of the castle church in Wittenberg in the eastern German state of Saxony and nailed to its wooden surface a paper listing ninety-five theses or statements that he was prepared to debate with all comers. In the world he lived in, placing posters in public places was the standard method of getting in touch with people with similar interests. Luther hoped to find others who shared his belief that the church had gone astray on some very important matters, especially in the growing practice of selling indulgences, which raised money for the church by promising a reduction of the time the dead must spend in purgatory. In his view, this teaching was new and thoroughly unbiblical. For example, Luther's twenty-seventh and twenty-eighth theses state:

> They preach only human doctrines who say that as soon as the money clinks into the money chest, the soul flies out of purgatory. It is certain that when money clinks in the money chest greed and avarice can be increased; but when the church intercedes, the result is in the hands of God alone.

Numbers thirty-five and thirty-six hold that

> they who teach that contrition is not necessary on the part of those who intend to buy souls out of purgatory or to buy confessional privileges preach unchristian doctrine. Any truly repentant Christian has a right to full remission of penalty and guilt, even without indulgence letters.

Such teachings, in other words, hampered the development of true faith in German parishes. Luther intended to foster debate about the whole indulgence trade in order to reform it and all the teachings surrounding it.

If a theologian today were to post an offer to debate on an electronic bulletin board, e-mails might fly fast and furious, but it is unlikely that this act would start a revolution. Luther's propositions, however, were the spark that ignited forces that were ready to be set off. Northern Europe was a powder keg primed to explode—and not only the church, but the whole political and economic structure of the continent. When the shock waves died down, there was no longer a united Christian church in western Europe. Only now, nearly five hundred years later, are the divided segments of the church beginning to find ways to come together again in common mission to the world and in service to the one Lord we worship.

For centuries Rome had been the center of Europe and the western part of the Mediterranean world; the bishop of Rome, the pope, was able to control the secular rulers of that vast area through the wealth that flowed into Rome from the churches. It is important to understand that the medieval papacy wielded enormous secular power. Not only did it have its own army, but when it called on secular rulers to provide additional forces, they were expected to respond. Failure to do so could be punished with excommunication, which meant not only eternal damnation but also deprivation of earthly power—their subjects no longer needed to obey and rulers could lose their thrones. Gradually, however, new nation-states had begun to form with rulers who were eager to assert themselves and keep their growing wealth for their own use. The merchants and traders of an expanding middle class were also ready to challenge the feudal structure of European society.

Then as now, it was not always clear whether the wars people fought were waged primarily over territory, wealth, or ideas. Two centuries before Luther, for example, national divisions had been strong enough to create separate papacies for the better part of a century, with one pope ruling in France and another in Italy. That division was ended by a council summoned in the fifteenth century to reform the church, but no real reforms were made. Now the pressures were too strong to control. Luther had not intended to divide the church or to provide German rulers with an excuse for political or economic changes, but his argument against the papacy's economic and political power encouraged dukes, barons, counts, mayors, and other rulers to support him in his effort to reform the church.

The new movement resulting from Luther's challenge took different forms in different areas of Europe. Sixteenth-century Germany was not one country but a patchwork quilt of states of widely different size and nature ruled by an assortment of secular and religious figures. In some of these states, Lutheranism became the established church, recognized and supported by the state, with all the advantages and disadvantages of that status: on the one hand, secular privileges, and on the other, a tendency toward lethargy and indifference resulting from the established church's sense of security. In other states Roman Catholicism retained control, and in still others, the Calvinist tradition took hold. For a while violence flared up, but eventually it was agreed that in matters of faith *cuius regio eius religio,* literally, "whose reign, his religion" or, more loosely, "the ruler's faith is the faith of the region." Consequently, Lutheranism was established for the most part in the various states of northern and central Germany and the Scandinavian countries while the Roman Catholic Church held on to the states of southern Germany. It is important to remember that the post-Reformation church in no way established the separation of church and state.

Beyond Germany, Lutheranism was adopted by the states bordering the Baltic Sea and by Iceland as well. Each of these states likewise had distinctive histories that produced churches with quite different characters. For the most part, these states adopted Lutheranism when the political and religious authorities decided to declare the end of papal power, whether to acquire economic advantage or to reform a church badly in need of renewal.

In those various states that followed Luther, the Augsburg Confession was adopted as the basic statement of faith. This was not a "confession" in the sense we use today in making an admission of sin, but rather a proclamation of faith offering a summary of the central tenets of reformed faith, including the theology of ministry, the sacraments, the nature of the church, monastic vows, civil government, and the whole process of justification and salvation. Philip Melanchthon, a younger colleague of Luther, was the primary author of the Augsburg Confession; although Luther himself had little direct hand in it, his ideas were at its core. A group of church and political leaders signed the statement in 1530 in Augsburg, Germany, as evidence of the legitimacy of their position, as part of a defense of their demands for change, and as the basis for what they had hoped would be a restored relationship with a reformed Roman Catholic Church.

After the German Reformation: Radicals, Rationalists, and Pietists

Not everyone in Germany was satisfied with the outcome of Luther's Reformation. The first half of the seventeenth century was marked by renewed violence, with religion often providing either the excuse or the cause. Once again, economic and political factors were involved in struggles that convulsed most of Europe from 1618 to 1648. The effort of the emperor Ferdinand to impose the Roman Catholic faith on parts of Germany and Austria was a central cause of the controversy, and the thirty-year struggle that resulted became known as The Wars of Religion. Though the nominal purpose was to reimpose Roman Catholicism, secular rulers were often willing to enter into relationships that enhanced their political position, such as Cardinal Richelieu of France's alliances with Dutch, Danish, and German Protestants to balance Spanish power. At the end of these wars, the rulers of the German states won full sovereignty and the right of each to decide the faith of their territory, but the price was high. Economies were destroyed and populations scattered; plague, pestilence, and famine swept the land. By some estimates, the population of Germany may have been reduced in those years by a third or more. Many had died, but many also had emigrated to America in search of peace and taken their various versions of a reformed faith with them.

In the midst of the chaos of these times, a number of Christians took refuge in pietism, which emphasized inward faith apart from any establishment of religion. The formal orthodoxy of the Lutheran Church seemed to them an inadequate expression of faith, and small devotional groups formed to study the Bible and to pray under the leadership of a Lutheran minister who hoped to revive the Lutheran Church named Philipp Jakob Spener. The movement gathered many followers in Germany, though it lacked consistent leadership and rejected fixed standards. Taking various forms in different places, pietism maintained a strong emphasis on a personal devotion to Jesus and on sin and redemption.

In the eighteenth century, the tension between the pietist societies and the established churches was aggravated by a growing confidence in the power of human reason. Worn out by the struggles of the seventeenth century and impressed with Newton's discovery of the law of planetary motion and other signs of scientific progress, many people began to imagine an objective, outer world governed by order and reason, even as pietists continued to turn inward to the emotional and subjective aspects of human life and faith. The tension between the established Lutheran churches and the pietist societies led to increasing divisions and even emigration of some groups to America to find freedom to worship in their own way.

Sometimes whole congregations under the leadership of their pastor packed up their belongings and moved to the new world, establishing communities in the newly opened areas of Pennsylvania, Ohio, Missouri, and beyond. Lutherans came from different states and countries and from a variety of backgrounds; they brought with them different languages and ethnic customs, which they had every intention of maintaining. Once in America, they were often even more divided from each other than they had been in Europe—divided not only by their differing heritages but also by the vast distances and challenges of their new country. Lutherans formed dozens of associations, or synods, reflecting both their ethnic origins and some of the unresolved theological controversies of Europe. To help preserve their identity, they were quick to build schools as well as churches, but slow to become involved in the social and political structures around them. It seemed to Lutherans that the government had little to do with them and that they would do best to avoid involvement in the political and social issues of a society in which they still felt no strong sense of ownership.

After the Revolution: Creating an American Lutheran Church

The American Revolution elicited a wide range of response from Lutherans. Some found it easy to accept the German-born English king, George III, as their ruler and to enlist in the loyalist cause. Hessian mercenary soldiers were also brought from Germany to serve with the royalist forces. Other Lutherans, however, saw the war as a struggle between English-speaking people in which they had no particular interest. At the end of the war, Lutherans were still few in number and dependent on support from the homeland. America remained a mission field for Lutherans well into the nineteenth century. Missionaries and funds were sent from Germany and Scandinavia to support the fledgling new world congregations. The flow of immigration that continued through the century in reaction to European wars kept ties strong between the old world and the new. Immigration and support from abroad undoubtedly strengthened American Lutheranism, but the continuing sense of ethnic identity that was encouraged by both these factors delayed the unifying of the church and the adoption of English as a common language. German and the Scandinavian languages continued to be spoken in many places well into the twentieth century.

Though there were attempts in the eighteenth century to unite American Lutherans, the results fell short of the dreams. Slowly, in the course of the nineteenth and twentieth centuries, Lutherans began to be successful in reaching out to each other, becoming involved in an English-speaking society, and coming together in a common witness to the world around them. The first task was to unite the various Lutheran synods that had formed along ethnic and doctrinal lines. A General Synod was formed in 1820 and by 1860 two-thirds of all American Lutherans were members. A General Council and a General Synod South united still other earlier groupings. Several mergers that occurred between 1918 and 1963 finally culminated in the formation of the Evangelical Lutheran Church in America (ELCA) in 1987. The Missouri Synod, conservative in theology and more cautious ecumenically, has remained separate, as have several other smaller groups.

It is important to notice the role played by the Association of Evangelical Lutheran Churches in the formation of the ELCA. In the early 1970s, the Missouri Synod became markedly more conservative in its theology. As a result, a number of the less conservative Missouri Synod parishes broke away to form the Association of Evangelical Lutheran Churches (AELC). Though relatively small, this group provided a major impetus for the formation of the ELCA. Thus the twentieth century ended with two major Lutheran bodies in the United States: the ELCA, with over five million members, and the Missouri Synod, with over two million members, are the home of the vast majority of American Lutherans.

The Reformation in England
When Luther nailed his theses to the cathedral door in Germany, it seemed at first that England, across the water, might remain uninvolved. King Henry VIII, who came to the throne of England in 1509, was bright and ambitious. He had no desire to attack the papacy directly as long as he could use it to his advantage; indeed, the king even wrote a book in opposition to Luther's teaching. But Henry had wars to fight with France and Spain, and wars cost money. Scattered across the realm of England were rich monastic foundations that had once been essential to England's economy and educational system. Times had changed, however; the monks were fewer in number and their great buildings and lands were hard to justify. The papal envoy knew this as well as Henry and was ready to work with him to close the monasteries and seize their wealth for Henry's purposes and his own.

So far, so good, but Henry also believed he needed a male heir to succeed him on the throne and his marriage had produced only one surviving child, his daughter Mary. It occurred to Henry that the fact that his marriage to Catherine of Aragon had been irregular—Pope Julius II had given him a dispensation to marry his deceased brother's wife, contrary to church law at the time—might be the cause of this failure. If his marriage were annulled, he would be able to marry again in hopes of producing a male heir. But since Pope Clement VII, a virtual prisoner of Catherine of Aragon's nephew, the emperor Charles V, was in no position to help the English king, Henry decided he had no choice but to proclaim an end to the pope's authority in England. Turning then to English authority, Henry was able to secure the annulment of his marriage from the newly appointed Archbishop of Canterbury, Thomas Cranmer. His marriage to Anne Boleyn produced yet another daughter, Elizabeth, but it was not until his third marriage to Jane Seymour that Henry finally had his desired male heir, who would become Edward VI.

Despite his challenge of the papacy, however, very little changed in the English church as long as Henry lived. An English translation of the Bible was authorized and two English-language prayers were inserted in the Latin mass, but that was as far as any efforts for reforms went. Henry died, however, before his son, Edward VI, was old enough to rule and Edward's advisors were much influenced by the Reformation Luther had begun in Germany. Archbishop Cranmer, who agreed with much that Luther taught, quickly provided a complete English prayer book in 1549; a revision printed three years later was much more deeply influenced by Reformation teaching.

Edward VI, however, was a sickly child and when he died in 1553 his older half-sister Mary came to the throne and attempted to restore Roman Catholicism in England. Known as "Bloody Mary," she severely persecuted those who resisted her will. After her death in 1559 people were glad to follow Mary's younger sister Elizabeth in a moderate reform that retained the structure of the pre-Reformation church while preserving freedom from Roman authority. The long reign of Elizabeth I, from 1558 to 1603, provided the opportunity for the reformed English church to become an accepted and familiar part of English life. It is interesting to note that through all the changes that took place under Henry, Edward, and Mary, the papacy took no final action to excommunicate English rulers or Christians. Not until Elizabeth had created a stable and continuing English church did Rome finally excommunicate her and so bring about a lasting separation between the two churches.

It is important to remember that in England, as in Germany, there was no separation of church and state. Society was a unified whole: the church taught the faith that the secular ruler and his or her subjects held and defended. Therefore to dissent from the established faith was to undermine the whole society; either everyone changed their faith or no one did. So England moved from being part of a European society in which the papacy defined the faith that all the secular rulers held, to being an independent state in which the king and Parliament protected a reformed faith, but church and state still remained united. Both in Germany and in England, moreover, a varied pattern of divisions was created by the interplay of economics, politics, and religion.

The king of England and the English church did, in fact, exercise control over most of the territory of the British Isles, but nationalistic forces in Scotland, Ireland, and Wales allied themselves with other churches as a way to express their own ethnic differences. In Scotland the reformed faith of John Calvin eventually emerged triumphant in the form of an established Presbyterian Church; in Wales the evangelistic efforts of John Wesley led to the emergence of the Methodist Church in the late eighteenth century as the majority faith of that country. In Ireland, the Roman Catholic Church allied itself with the national fervor of the Irish and emerged from long years of persecution as the faith of the great majority except in the northeast. There, immigration from Scotland sponsored by the English government produced a protestant majority and sowed the seeds of a bitter conflict that has not yet been resolved. Anglicanism survived in all these areas as a minority faith, but one very much aware of what made it different from the majority. Thus in Scotland and Wales, Anglicanism has tended to emphasize its catholic heritage, while in Ireland its protestant character is foremost. Today there are Anglican churches in each of these four countries—the Church of England, the Church of Ireland, the Church of Wales, and the Episcopal Church of Scotland—each with a distinctive history and character.

Further Divisions and Conflict in Anglicanism
There were, almost inevitably, many in England who were not content with Elizabeth's reformation settlement and who sought more radical changes. When James I came to the throne in 1603, the Puritan party petitioned for drastic changes in the established church, asking that the making of the sign of the cross in baptism, the blessing and giving of a ring in marriage, the wearing of surplices, and the rite of confir-

mation all be eliminated. Dissenters also sought
changes in the Catechism and the Articles of Religion
and the abolition of distinctions between bishops and
priests. When no change was forthcoming, some dissenters took refuge first in Holland and then in New
England. Pressure for change in England itself continued, however, and finally a civil war erupted that
ended with the execution of King Charles I in 1649
and the establishment of a commonwealth ruled by
Oliver Cromwell and a Puritan Parliament. But the
English people liked the excessive austerity of Puritan
rule no better than the excessive harshness of Mary.
When Cromwell died, they gladly welcomed the king's
son, Charles II, back from France; he brought back
with him the bishops and prayer book of the established Church of England.

The turbulence of the seventeenth century gave
way to an eighteenth century in which the English
people, like the German people, were ready for a season of peace. At a time when Isaac Newton and other
scientists were opening up a whole new understanding
of the world and the laws of nature, it began to seem
that the universe was as systematic and orderly as a
clock. God could be understood as a clockmaker, the
Creator of a rational cosmos in which the stars and
planets revolved in their courses and human beings
needed only to understand this system for all to be well.
Historians of the period speak of the "Age of Reason"
and the "Enlightenment." Some theologians wrote of
God in those terms and of religion as "not mysteri-
ous."

New Englanders, for whom that vision of the world
fit well with their striving for simplicity in worship,
built themselves churches painted white within and
without and put clear glass in the windows as expressions of their new vision of the simple clarity of both

the Christian faith and of human reason and progress. This architecture reflects several elements that would leave a deep impression on American religion: a fear of superstition and religious authoritarianism, an affirmation of enlightenment philosophy, and a focus on preaching rather than the sacraments. In Germany and England alike, secular rulers found much to appreciate in this type of faith; it caused less trouble and provided useful support for stability and social order.

The emotional pietism that had flourished in Germany after the Wars of Religion spread to England, especially through the preaching of John Wesley. A priest of the Church of England, Wesley was raised in a clergy family and educated at Oxford, but he came in contact with a group of European immigrants who had been influenced by German pietism. He went one day to a meeting at which the preface to Luther's *Commentary on the Epistle to the Romans* was being read, and as he listened he found his heart "strangely warmed." He went on to become a leader in English evangelicalism with a particular mission to the laborers in the industrial areas of England and the coal mines of Wales. They, in turn, responded to a kind of preaching that brought drama and purpose to the stark poverty of their lives. Yet just as in Germany at that time, so in England the tension between a rationalistic state church and emotional evangelicalism led finally to divisions that could not be bridged. The Methodist societies of Wesley became at last a separate church, just as many of the German pietists formed bodies separate from the state churches.

The Colonial Period
In the new world, Anglican church life developed differently in the three primary areas of English settle-

ment: the southern colonies, the middle colonies, and New England. In the south, especially in Virginia, the English church was established by law as it had been in England. In theory everything was the same; in practice, however, local church life was very different since king, Parliament, and bishops were far away. Lacking the structure of English church and civil government, the colonists created new structures that not only preserved the unity of church and state but made it in some ways even stronger. In Virginia, the governor served as both king and bishop while the elected House of Burgesses substituted for the Parliament and church assembly; lay vestries administered the church and government in each local community. What that meant, of course, was that clergy were hired by vestries and subject to their authority, circumstances that could only reinforce the tendencies of the church in that age toward rationalism and the avoidance of theological controversy. More positively, it gave the laity an extraordinarily large voice in the governing of the church and helped to prepare the way for changes in church life after the American Revolution.

New England, on the other hand, was settled first of all by immigrants who came determined to escape from the established Church of England and carry out a more thorough reformation similar to that of John Calvin and the Reformed churches of Switzerland, Holland, and Scotland. Arriving in Massachusetts, they put in place an established church of their own that had no place for bishops, prayer books, or any of the outward and visible aspects of church life identified with Rome and medieval corruption. As intolerant of other viewpoints as the established church had been of them, they drove out free-thinkers and religious dissidents like Roger Williams and Anne Hutchinson. The New England colonists, however, had to coexist eventually with representatives of the established church since their charter for settlement came from the English government. When conditions in England became more stable, priests of the Church of England arrived in New England and gradually a small but definite presence of the English church grew up in the midst of the Puritan commonwealth. By the eighteenth century, Anglicans had won the right to withhold their taxes from the Puritan church and even to have their taxes used to support their own church.

Needing to fight for survival with the reformed establishment, Anglicans in New England reacted by emphasizing the things that made them different from the Puritans: bishops, liturgy, and sacraments. In an age of rationalism, New England Anglicans were drawn back to the ancient and catholic aspects of their faith. They had little in common with their Virginia counterparts apart from using the same *Book of Common Prayer* and praying for the same king.

Circumstances in the middle colonies (Maryland, Pennsylvania, and New York) were very different from those in New England. Since these also were areas of English settlement, the Anglican church was eventually established, though not so completely as in Virginia since other religious groups were strongly represented: Roman Catholicism in Maryland, for example, Quakers in Pennsylvania, and the Dutch Reformed Church in New York. One interesting aspect of the experience of the middle colonies was the attempt to develop Swedish settlements in Delaware and Pennsylvania. The Swedish government, however, did not provide resources to support the effort and eventually left them on their own. Believing that there was no significant difference between their inherited faith and that of the English settlers around them, the Swedes who stayed became part of the Church of

England and then, after the Revolution, of the Episcopal Church. Some Episcopal churches in this area are known to this day as "Old Swedes Church" in recognition of that heritage.

After the Revolution, Anglicans lost the privileged position they had held in most of the colonies as well as the support of English missionary societies in New England. Since before the war their clergy had been required to take an oath of loyalty and pray for the King of England, many fled to Canada while their churches were closed or burned. When the war was over, it seemed to many that the remnants of the church would die out within one generation. That it did not was the result of the inspiration of a remarkable generation of new leaders who helped the church rebuild in the nineteenth century and discover a new identity in a new country.

Even this new identity, however, has its roots in the patterns from which it emerged. For example, Anglicans still assumed that they were members of one church and that the church they belonged to must have bishops. How to get them was another question, since only bishops can consecrate another bishop. William White, one of the leading clergy of Philadelphia, suggested that bishops might be created instead by the laying on of priests' hands. New England Anglicans, however, would not accept such an idea and sent one of their number, Samuel Seabury, to England to seek a proper consecration by bishops. Unable to take the required oath of loyalty to the crown, Seabury journeyed in 1784 to Scotland, where Anglican bishops understood the problems of a minority church and required no oath of loyalty. With that precedent established, the Church of England then made provision to consecrate bishops without an oath of loyalty to the royal authority and bishops were consecrated for New York, Pennsylvania, and Virginia. The name "Protestant Episcopal" was chosen to indicate the reformed catholic nature of the church, a General Convention was created to provide church government, and the church had an identity and a structure with which to face the future.

Toward Christian Unity
Where Lutherans developed a strong system of parish schools to propagate their faith and preserve their ethnic heritage, Episcopalians developed the New England preparatory schools not so much to propagate their faith as to shape their offspring for the leadership roles they assumed were rightfully theirs. Recovering from the Revolution and reaching out in mission to the new lands in the west, the Episcopal Church throughout the nineteenth century imagined itself to be the future of American Christianity. While its New England schools educated the sons of the wealthy, the church also developed a social conscience that sent priests into the poor neighborhoods of major cities to work with newly arrived immigrants and industrial workers. The first wave of liturgical reform and the Darwinian challenge to biblical authority stretched the church almost to the breaking point, but the strength of a common prayer book helped to overcome these tensions.

Although lay Episcopalians often held positions of political and social prominence in nineteenth-century America, the church itself was far from dominant. While Episcopalians were solidifying their hold on the traditional establishment, Methodists and Baptists spread rapidly in the south and west, and new immigrant groups—Roman Catholics and Lutherans in particular—gradually learned to speak English and wield the levers of democracy. By the middle of the twentieth

century it was clear that the churches of the old establishment—Episcopalians, Methodists, Presbyterians,
and Congregationalists—no longer spoke for the
mainstream of American Christianity.

Nevertheless, it was the Episcopal Church, out of
its assumption of national leadership, that gave the
first impetus to the ecumenical movement in the nineteenth century. In 1886 a proposal made by an
Episcopal priest from New York, William Reed
Huntington, was adopted first by the General
Convention of the Episcopal Church and then by the
Lambeth Conference of bishops of the Anglican
Communion. The Lambeth Quadrilateral set out four
elements as essential to the restoration of visible
Christian unity: the Bible, the historic creeds, the two
sacraments of baptism and Holy Communion, and the
historic episcopate. In 1927, moreover, an Episcopal
bishop, Charles Henry Brent, called for and presided
over the first session of the World Conference on Faith
and Order. After World War II, it was Bishop James
Pike who cooperated with Presbyterian Eugene Carson
Blake to initiate conversations that finally involved a
number of major American churches in negotiations
toward church unity. While these produced significant
proposals and fostered a deeper understanding, they
also clarified divisions over the nature of the ministry,
sacraments, and scriptural authority that were not to
be overcome easily.

Ultimately, however, it was the Evangelical
Lutheran Church in America (ELCA), perhaps
because it had learned so much from its own struggle
for unity among Lutherans, that stood at the center of
the most significant ecumenical developments at the
turn of the century. The pathway it followed was not
one of church merger but rather of mutual recognition and intercommunion. Agreements involving full

communion and mutual recognition of ministries were developed not only with the Episcopal Church, but also with the United Church of Christ, the Reformed Church in America and the Presbyterian Church (USA) (churches of the Reformed or Calvinist tradition), and the northern and southern provinces of the Moravian Church. Called to Common Mission (CCM), was adopted in 1999 by the Evangelical Lutheran Church in America and in 2000 by the Episcopal Church. This last agreement was perhaps the most significant, involving as it did the adoption of the historic episcopate by the ELCA. The hope is that this agreement will give visible and liturgical form to the unity we already have in Christ. Similar agreements between Anglican and Lutheran churches are developing in Europe and Africa as well.

As we stand at the dawn of a new century and new relationship and look back, what may be most noteworthy for Lutherans and Episcopalians is the way our histories have intertwined through four and a half centuries and been molded by similar forces. Luther's influence helped shape the English Reformation and the development of *The Book of Common Prayer.* John Wesley was also deeply influenced by Luther, and Wesley in turn influenced German pietism. The same forces of rationalism and pietism had an impact on English and German Christianity in the seventeenth and eighteenth centuries. Both churches were forced to work out new identities for themselves in North America against the influence of the industrial revolution and the Darwinian revolution; both churches have taken leadership roles in the struggle for Christian unity.

The movement toward Christian unity has several foundations. More and more Christians are realizing in a practical sense how much more effective the churches can be when they are working together and in a theological sense how scandalous Christian divisions are in the light of Christ's prayer that his followers might be one. For Anglicans, the inherited memory of a unified state church may lie behind the desire to unite Christians in a common pattern of worship. For Lutherans, the pain of past division working against the counterpoint of the successful uniting of many synods has deepened their inclination toward a greater unity beyond the Lutheran family. The adoption by both churches of Called to Common Mission puts them in a position to move into the new century with new strength. The response of individual church members and congregations to this opportunity will determine whether or not the Christian church can once again bear united witness to its risen Lord for the benefit of the whole society in which it is called to serve. All this is in truth a fulfillment of the dreams of those who first set out to reform and renew the church nearly five centuries ago.

For Reflection

What denomination(s) have been part of your life or the lives of members of your family?

Why did you change from one denomination to another or what led you to stay in one denomination without changing? What drew you to one church or turned you away from another?

CHAPTER TWO

WHAT WE BELIEVE

The Role of Theology and Tradition

As we human beings come to know God, we try to put that knowledge into words and music and art and all the other means by which we have learned to express ourselves. Words are an essential tool for human self-expression but they have their limits because human understanding has its limits. It is not surprising, therefore, that some traditions have placed more value on theology than others and that different churches have used it in very different ways. Lutherans and Anglicans, for example, demonstrate two distinct approaches to theology, perhaps because of the unique circumstances that formed these two traditions. Theology never exists in a vacuum: historical events as well as personalities often play a role in shaping the ways we think. This is most certainly the case in the development of theology in the Lutheran and Anglican strands of the Christian tradition. In order to see the distinctions more clearly, it will be helpful to look first at the ways in which Anglicans and Lutherans have done theology and then at some of the primary topics they have dealt with.

The Lutheran Approach

Martin Luther was a theologian by training. He was a monk, a priest, and a professor. When he challenged the church authorities of his day by posting his ninety-five theses on the cathedral door, he was raising theological questions. Luther's hope was that these theses would be debated by other theologically trained church leaders. It is no surprise, then, that both his opponents and his supporters used theological language and methods.

As the German Reformation took shape, a number of carefully written documents were issued stating the theological positions the reformers held. These documents were intended to demonstrate that the questions raised by Luther and his supporters did not set them outside the traditional catholic faith and could not be used as grounds for excommunication. The first major document in this collection is called the Augsburg Confession (1530). Because the Augsburg Confession remains a central pillar of Lutheran theology, it is worth describing this document in some detail.

First, the confession covers beliefs about which there was no disagreement, such as the trinitarian nature of God, the canon of scripture, and the use of the sacraments. These articles were intended to establish the common ground between the papal and reformed sides, and to assert the unbroken link between Lutheran teaching and the ancient church. The confession then discusses practices about which there was a divergence of opinion, including clergy marriage, the power of bishops, monastic vows, and the mass. It claims that Lutheran practices in these areas cannot be legitimately forbidden, because they are matters of Christian freedom, or even Christian obligation. For example, the giving of both bread and wine at communion was not allowed by Rome in Luther's day but he and his followers defended the distribution "in both kinds" by biblical and canonical precedent.

Perhaps the most important theological statements in the Augsburg Confession were the two articles defining justification and the church. Justification is described as equivalent to forgiveness; it means we are enabled to stand before God in righteousness. According to the confession, the Bible teaches that we are justified by God's grace apart from any works or deeds of our own. We receive this gift of justification by faith: that is, we simply trust in God's great mercy to grant such a gift. This teaching does not negate the need for good works in the Christian life, but good works become a response to God's love and grace, not a prerequisite for forgiveness. For example, we no longer attend mass on holy days, fast, or give alms in order to merit God's love or mercy, but we now do them to show our joy and gratitude to such a gracious God. For some Christians, this teaching was a radical change that lifted the burdens of endless religious obligations and restored joy to the Christian life.

The article defining the church was likewise startling to many Christians in Luther's day. The Augsburg Confession states that the church "is the assembly of believers among whom the Gospel is preached in its purity and the holy sacraments are administered according to the Gospel." This definition does not mention bishops, priests, orders, dogmas, or traditions; it puts the emphasis squarely on the gathered laity, who, with their clergy, celebrate and receive gladly the grace of God in both word and sacrament. This description of the church is intended to reflect the New Testament picture of a "holy nation" and a "royal priesthood" that includes the entire body of Christian believers. It does not reject the role of ordained clergy, nor the utility of well-ordered structure, but it lifts up the gathered faithful as the fullest manifestation of the church, rather than the clergy.

The Augsburg Confession was followed in 1531 by the Apology of the Augsburg Confession, written to provide an extended explanation of the original document and to clear up some areas of uncertainty. Still later came the Schmalkald Articles (1537), the Treatise on the Power and Primacy of the Pope (1537), and finally, thirty-one years after Martin Luther's death, the Formula of Concord (1577). These were then combined with the "Three Chief Symbols" (the Apostles' Creed, the Nicene Creed, and the Athanasian Creed), and Luther's *Small* and *Large Catechisms* (1529) to make the *Book of Concord*. This book of Reformation era writings defines the movement which, against Martin Luther's will, had come to be known as Lutheranism. The documents contain no official liturgy and no clearly defined church structure. Their essence is the statement that all people depend entirely upon God's grace as we receive it in Jesus Christ, that we are justified by grace through faith, and that the true church exists wherever believers hear the gospel purely preached and receive the sacraments properly administered. Scripture alone, faith alone, and grace alone were the watchwords of this movement for reform. They make the claim that these elements, when properly understood, have always been at the heart of the church's teaching. Therefore, Lutherans see themselves as being part of the church continuing the authentic apostolic tradition.

On the whole, the reformers were conservative, holding on to as much of the inherited tradition as they felt they could. The very word "reform" indicates an intention to modify what already exists, not to begin something totally new. But the continental reformers insisted that the details of church structure and worship were not mandated by scripture and therefore could not be legitimately required by any bishops or councils, or even by the weight of tradition.

In the centuries following the German Reformation Lutherans have continued to take theology seriously. Their theological method has remained the same: define the issue being studied, examine it from the perspective of the scriptures, test it against the Lutheran confessions, make sure the doctrine of justification in Christ is clear, and then offer that teaching to the church.

The Anglican Approach
Anglican theology developed in an entirely different context. Though the English Parliament decreed an end to papal authority, the English church claimed to remain part of the authentic apostolic tradition. It based this claim on the church's continuation of the traditional pattern of ministry, along with the liturgy and ancient creeds. Like Luther and his followers, the English reformers and political leaders did not intend to create a new church. For Henry VIII and his supporters, this was a decision about jurisdiction and authority, not about the ancient faith of the church.

They believed (as Lutherans also do) that the bond of unity in Christ had been present before the claims of papal jurisdiction had been made, and would remain even after the Church of England began to select its own bishops and priests. This belief assumes that matters such as the territory over which the bishop of Rome can claim authority are not central to the life and faith of the Body of Christ—the same position taken five hundred years earlier, when the patriarch of the eastern churches refused to accept the papal claim of universal primacy, leading to the division between the eastern and western churches that continues to this day.

Every Christian tradition recognizes the need, even the divine mandate, for some system of ministry and oversight within the life of the church. However, the western reformers of the sixteenth century, echoing the position of the Orthodox churches from the eleventh century, maintained that the papal claim of universal jurisdiction went beyond the early church's understanding of the ministry of oversight, and was not essential to the life of the church.

It must be emphasized that the English church was not, in the beginning at least, resisting the papacy on theological issues. Indeed, Henry VIII had written a book challenging Luther's theology of the sacraments and had been awarded the title "Defender of the Faith" by Pope Leo X. The issue between England and Rome was one of authority alone. Since the Church of England did not consider itself to be involved in any kind of doctrinal debate with the western Christian tradition, it had no need to spell out its beliefs in a new creed or confession except to maintain its essential continuity with western tradition.

The Thirty-Nine Articles of Religion, often considered the closest document Anglicans have to a doctrinal statement, was not issued until 1571, soon after the pope had denounced Queen Elizabeth as an illegitimate usurper of the throne and thus had forced English Christians to choose between loyalty to the papacy or the crown. A central point of the articles was to affirm that the pope had no jurisdiction in England. Echoes of Luther and Calvin can be found in their language but they were never used in the same way as the Lutheran and Calvinist confessions of faith. The articles were not intended to be precise and narrow definitions of doctrine but broad and inclusive statements of the Christian tradition. Jeremy Taylor, an influential Anglican bishop and theologian in the seventeenth century, noted that the articles had been "framed with much caution and prudence, and so as might abstain from grieving the contrary minds of differing men." Not until the eighteenth century were the articles even published in the prayer book. The 1979 American edition of *The Book of Common Prayer* includes the Thirty-Nine Articles in a section called merely "Historical Documents."

For Henry, Cranmer, and other English reformers the central issue was not so much doctrine as the authority of the bishop of Rome, which they held was of no greater weight than that of any other foreign bishop. When they claimed the authority to choose the leadership within the Church of England, they believed they were not attacking or amending any ancient doctrine or practice. The struggle over the right to make practical decisions for the life of the church—such as setting diocesan boundaries and selecting clergy for various positions—had roots deep in the Middle Ages. Popes and kings had fought over these powers for centuries. *Magna Carta,* the famous declaration of English freedom won from King John by the barons and nobles in 1215, asserted also the freedom of the Church of England. Papal authority had waxed and waned over the centuries; the English reformers simply set out to establish clear limits to that authority in their own day. Changes of this sort, they argued, can be made for the practical life of the church, but the apostolic faith, as witnessed in the scriptures, the liturgy, and the early creeds and councils, was to be maintained as it had always been.

Unlike Luther's followers, reformers in England were in position to balance the authority of the pope with the authority of the king. That done, they could proceed more slowly to amend and modify inherited patterns of church life, adopting ideas of Luther's and Calvin's as they chose, but never needing to create a complete new theological structure. But if, as many Anglicans would claim, there is no distinctive Anglican theological system, it is possible nevertheless to describe an Anglican method summed up in the Latin phrase *lex orandi, lex credendi* (the rule of prayer is the rule of belief). In other words, beliefs are established through worship. It is through worship that we come to know who God is, and our theology is shaped by that experience.

Anglicans, a term that includes members of the Episcopal Church in the United States, believe that Christian worship, properly ordered according to the prayer book pattern, contains the essential elements of the faith and that we will come to understand that faith as we worship. Anglicans hold that the Holy Eucharist and other central services such as baptism and ordination, along with the daily offices of Morning and Evening Prayer, with their systematic reading of the scriptures in a context of prayer, express the core of Christian teaching. These liturgies not only refer frequently to the Trinity, to sin and forgiveness, to Christ's life, death, and resurrection, and to our mission to love our neighbors, but also enable worshipers to act out their faith in a concentrated and carefully ordered pattern. The liturgy then becomes an ongoing educational process, in which the gifts of God are received and offered and the lives of the worshipers are shaped. Theological formulations often emerge from this common experience of worship, but it is the worship that shapes the theology, not the theology that shapes the worship.

It is worth noting in this respect that the agreement between the Episcopal and Lutheran churches, Called to Common Mission (CCM), does not provide an agreed theological statement about episcopacy; rather, it simply creates a procedure to be used hereafter in the installation of bishops. A common liturgical pattern is set in place and provides a powerful witness to the unity of faith we have found, but the churches remain free to hold various perspectives on the importance of the historic succession of bishops. Episcopalians find in the liturgy the essential expression of unity in faith; for Lutherans, agreement in doctrine is primary. Lutherans take their confessions (understood as restatements of biblical and apostolic teaching) as the norm, while liturgies are developed as unofficial expressions of the faith and never supercede the confessions as vehicles for expressing the faith. Lutherans promise allegiance to a confession of faith; Episcopalians swear to uphold a pattern of worship. And yet because the agreements summarized in Called to Common Mission have grown out of over thirty years of theological study, a common liturgical expression has become both possible and desirable.

Questions of Authority
Since its earliest beginnings there have been disagreements and even divisions in the Christian church.

Questioning and debate seem to be necessary for us to work out clearer understandings of what we believe and practice. Ideally, the process leads to a common mind; unfortunately it may also lead to schism. Faced with controversy, the early Christians developed several methods for clarifying the church's teaching. At the beginning they turned naturally to the apostles as the source of authority, and when the apostles disagreed they came together to discuss their differences and reach agreement. Acts 15, for example, tells of one such council held in Jerusalem to consider whether Gentile converts needed to accept the Jewish law. When the apostles died and could no longer be consulted directly, Christians assembled the writings they had received from the apostles and turned to these documents for guidance. They also looked to those who were believed to have been chosen by the apostles as their successors, people who came to be called bishops. The bishops, as successors to the apostles, were considered authorities on the apostles' teaching, and bishops of the larger and older churches won places of special respect and leadership. Over the centuries, the bishop of Rome, who oversaw the only significant church in the western Mediterranean world, won a dominant place for himself in the western church, claiming his authority to come primarily from the apostle Peter, who was believed to have died in Rome as a martyr.

When Luther challenged the authority of the pope in the sixteenth century, he was, in effect, rejecting the authority of the apostles' successor and turning instead to the authority of the apostles' writings alone. Rome, in reaction, added new weight to the authority of the pope until, in the nineteenth century, he was declared to be infallible when speaking *ex cathedra* (from his throne) on matters of faith and order.

Protestants, in response, have tended to exalt still further the authority of scripture until, in the twentieth century, fundamentalists have declared the scriptures infallible even in dealing with matters like creation and evolution.

Luther, on the other hand, had adopted a nuanced view of scripture, and even went so far as to speak of the letter of James as an "epistle of straw." He likened the Bible to the manger at Bethlehem in which the Christ Child lay. The manger had value as holding the Holy Child, but the Child was more important than its bedding. Lutherans, as a result, focus on what they call the gospel. The gospel is not simply the biography of Jesus as told in the gospels, but is the sum of the promises and gifts of God to sinful humanity. The gospel is the word of grace—God's unmerited love and mercy—to a fallen world. It can be found throughout the Bible but is most fully received in the person of Jesus Christ. He is seen as the "Word made flesh"—the ultimate expression of God's will for all humankind. For Lutherans, the gospel is the "canon within the canon," meaning that the whole of scripture (and tradition, too) can only be properly understood from the perspective of the gospel.

While Lutherans interpret the Bible in terms of the gospel at its heart, Anglicans tend to interpret the Bible in the light of the teachings of the early church. The English reformers asked how the early church had interpreted the scriptures. They studied the first Christian theologians, known as "the church fathers," and the documents issued by ecumenical (meaning worldwide or all-inclusive) councils that were held in the fourth and fifth centuries—including the Nicene Creed as a definitive summary of the Christian faith. Referring primarily to these writings as the "tradition" and stressing the vital role of human reason in interpreting the faith, they came to speak of a threefold source of authority: scripture, tradition, and reason. The common image of a "three-legged stool" is sometimes misunderstood to imply that there are three separate *and* *equal* authorities on which Anglican authority rests, but scripture remains fundamental. Those ordained in the Episcopal Church are asked to declare that they "do believe the Holy Scriptures of the Old and New Testaments to be the Word of God, and to contain all things necessary to salvation" (*The Book of Common Prayer,* 513). Tradition and reason are simply aids to interpreting and understanding the scripture. Anglicans would argue that the scriptures are not a clearly self-evident authority or there would be no differences of opinion about their interpretation. Tradition, which includes the whole life and witness of the church through the ages, must therefore be consulted; otherwise, each Christian would be left to his or her own opinion and we might easily have as many churches as Christians.

Luther and his followers did not deny the value of reason and experience, but they were convinced that neither reason nor experience could lead anyone to trust fully in God's grace. Finally, that trust must be what the nineteenth century Danish theologian Søren Kierkegaard called a "leap of faith." Because Lutherans teach that both reason and experience are susceptible to corruption by sin, they speak of *sola fide* (faith alone). The Word of God, incarnate in Christ, written in scripture, proclaimed from the pulpit and made visible in baptism and communion, is the true word of life. It creates what it promises—forgiveness and abundant life for all who receive it. Faith is trust in this Word and its power to bring about a new creation.

In the same way, while Lutherans acknowledge the movement of the Holy Spirit within the church since New Testament times, they insist that the only trustworthy test of the faithfulness of the church's life and teaching is the Bible. In using the phrase *sola scriptura* (scripture alone) they do not mean to reject or deny other sources of authority, but the Lutheran notion of sin is very deep and they are therefore cautious about identifying any human institution, including the church, with the kingdom of God. Lutherans also focus on what Martin Luther called the "theology of the cross." As a counterpoint to the triumphalism or concentration on power that may corrupt powerful churches, like the Roman church of Luther's day, Lutherans tend to see the crucifixion as the defeat of death in the willing suffering of Christ. To follow him means to "take up our cross" rather than to bask in his glory.

The Meaning of Faith
Lutheranism may be seen as having developed out of one man's private religious struggle and resulting insight. Wrestling with doubt about his own salvation, Luther was suddenly filled with new hope while reading Paul's letter to the Romans. There he read: "For we hold that a person is justified by faith apart from works prescribed by the law" (3:28). He began to notice this theme all through the Bible, especially in the New Testament, and it became the key that unlocked a new and deeper understanding of God's purpose. The idea that sinners could be made righteous (or put in a right relationship with God) because of their trust in God's promises is at the heart of the Lutheran witness. This is the meaning of the third Lutheran *sola*: *sola gratia* (grace alone). No matter what we achieve, avoid, or accomplish, our deeds or

"good works" can never be the basis for our justification. This would make God a paymaster rewarding laborers for their productive efforts. Even worse, if taken to its extreme, any reliance on our own works could seem to make Christ superfluous. Rather, Lutherans hold that the life of faith is the joyful reception of a most generous gift from God in Christ. Having received this blessing, we then go out to share it in word and deed with our neighbors.

The Anglican understanding of the Christian faith, by contrast, did not develop out of an individual's struggle and insight but out of the life of a whole national church set free from Roman authority. The private struggle with sin has been less central to Anglicanism than an emphasis on God's goodness in creation. If the Bible can be summed up in the great themes of creation and the fall in the Old Testament and incarnation and redemption in the New Testament, it may be true to say that Anglicans have tended to stress creation and incarnation while Lutherans have stressed the fall and redemption. Such a statement, inevitably, is a vast oversimplification. There have always been Anglicans who have centered their faith on sin and redemption, and there have been times in which that emphasis has been dominant in Anglicanism. John Newton, a priest in the Church of England, wrote the words to the hymn "Amazing grace! how sweet the sound, that saved a wretch like me!"; it was also an Anglican who wrote the words to another well-known hymn, "All things bright and beautiful, all creatures great and small, all things wise and wonderful, the Lord God made them all."

In Anglicanism the creation, which God declared "good," the making of humanity in God's image, and the joining together of humanity and divinity in the incarnation of Jesus all form the framework for the life-transforming human encounter with divine grace and glory. Just as the incarnation of the Second Person of the Trinity in Jesus, the son of Mary, is central to Anglican worship, so the incarnation is reflected also in the Anglican understanding of the church and the sacraments. The church, the great body of Christians through the ages, is itself understood to be an expression of divine incarnation as the Holy Spirit guides and refines its life and mission, and the sacramental elements of water, bread, and wine are seen as bearers of divine grace. Incarnation, church, and sacramental worship fit logically together. Those who place a high emphasis on this understanding of church and sacraments have been called "high church," while those placing more value on preaching and evangelism have been called "low church." All Anglicans, however, value church and sacrament more highly than most of the reformed churches. Some of these themes are also found in the Orthodox churches of the east, whose theology has had an early and continuing influence on Anglican thought.

As a liturgical church and one established by law in England, Anglicans are even more inclined to "good order" than their very orderly Lutheran colleagues. They believe that God will work through the gathered community in worship to bring true faith and fellowship, and to produce true righteousness. They prefer on the whole not to express themselves in a series of *solas*. They would rather embrace the richness and variety of tradition as well as the theology that can flow from it. They are somewhat suspicious of the idea that any one age or one theologian or one theological school can produce the final, definitive, or absolutely normative statement of the faith. Anglicans have come to see that the Lutheran confessions can be valid expressions of the faith and to accept Lutheranism as a legitimate strand within the Holy Catholic Church, but they generally believe that the faith is best preserved and commended to others through forms of worship and ministry in substantial continuity with those of the early church.

Lutheran theology may not stress the incarnation in the same way as Anglicans, but it is nevertheless thoroughly Christ-centered. Jesus Christ and the redemption we receive through his death and resurrection are at the center of Lutheran preaching and teaching. While understanding the fullness of the Trinity and gladly calling upon the Father, Son, and Holy Spirit in worship and prayer, Lutheranism is a very concrete tradition. Lutherans believe that the Father can only truly be known through the Son (Augsburg Confession, Article XX), and that one of the most important works of the Holy Spirit is to call us to faith in the Son (*Small Catechism*). It is Jesus Christ and his justifying death on our behalf that forms the focal point for faith and spirituality in Lutheranism.

Toward a New Consensus
The Episcopal Church in the United States, like many other Christian bodies, has been undergoing a transition in recent decades, as ecumenical discussions and debates have stimulated serious reevaluations of both the nature and content of the Christian faith. Two currents of reform are clear. The first is a continuing effort to update the language of the prayer book for contemporary worshipers. The other is a renewal of ministry and liturgy drawn from a deeper understanding of the first centuries of the church's life. Over the last half of the twentieth century, the celebration of the Holy Eucharist has become, as in the early church, the normal pattern of worship on Sunday mornings. The

permanent, ordained diaconate, as part of a threefold ordering of ministries rather than a transitional introduction to priesthood, has been recovered. Baptism has become at last, as Archbishop Thomas Cranmer intended it to be, a familiar part of communal worship rather than a private ceremony.

These changes are not just adjustments in practice; they reflect a shift in theology. The life-changing salvation of God is to be found in ancient teachings and practices, but it must be presented to modern people without archaic vocabulary or obscure ceremonies. The Anglican tradition assumes that the road to unity is to be found in common worship. Christian unity is a stated goal of most Christian people and most Christian churches. For Episcopalians, that unity will be of a practical nature. It will consist of Christians who hold a wide variety of opinions and who are bound together in a commonly accepted structure of ministry and oversight worshiping together in ways that reflect the ancient practices of the church. Specific doctrinal details may shift or be redefined, but the central mystery of salvation will continue to be embedded in the traditional forms of worship and maintained by a traditional church order.

Lutherans also value and seek Christian unity. But they have championed the view that the true unity of the church is to be found in "the gospel rightly preached and the sacraments properly administered." This means that for Lutherans, doctrinal agreement both precedes and undergirds all movements toward Christian unity. While other Christians need not "sign on" in a formal way to the Augsburg Confession or the *Book of Concord*, Lutherans must be able to see the gospel, as they understand it, within any tradition with which they will enter full communion. Despite different emphases and methodology, Lutherans have recognized within Anglicanism the essential elements of faith that make full communion not only possible but desirable. The ordered ministry as a gift from God, the sacraments of baptism and eucharist as effective signs of grace, the dependence upon the work of Christ for salvation, and the reliance upon scriptures and ancient creeds all proclaim the kind of common tradition that would seem to call for further steps toward visible unity.

Though recognizing differences in structures and "personality," Anglicans likewise have seen in Lutheranism the central deposit of the apostolic tradition. As an inheritor and transmitter of the ancient faith, Lutherans are now viewed as true partners to Anglicans in a worldwide mission. Movements toward full communion are therefore a faithful next step in their relationship.

We can see now, from the perspective of five hundred years of experience, that neither Lutheran nor Anglican assumptions have been effective in practice. Lutherans have been unable to unite even with other Lutherans around the Augsburg Confession, and Anglican organization and liturgy have not been able to prevent schisms (such as the Methodist movement) or to restore a broader Christian unity. Indeed, the Anglican insistence on an episcopal ministry in apostolic succession as a basis for Christian unity has led to great difficulties in the Consultation on Church Union (COCU) negotiations, now nearly a half-century old. Yet both Lutherans and Anglicans have found themselves to be part of a growing consensus among Christians that there is a way to do theology that draws from the best insights of various traditions and that enriches all parties. This is not what some have called "lowest common denominator" ecumenism. The new consensus is not based on removing all the distinctive marks of each tradition in order to create a minimal-istic, compromise version of the faith. Rather, we are seeing a new willingness to listen carefully to what each tradition has to say and why it is important to say it. Where one strand of the Christian church can bor-row from another, it may—and probably should—do so. But the heart of each tradition remains intact, offering a particular emphasis that a reunited church will need in order to remain true to its calling.

For Reflection

What is your image of God? Where do you think God is? What is God's nature (loving, angry, sorrowful, compas-sionate, joyful)?

How is God known to you? How has your denomination(s) taught you about God?

CHAPTER THREE

HOW WE WORSHIP

Changing Perspectives on Liturgy

History and theology may have played a major role in shaping the Lutheran and Episcopal Churches, but the ways in which we worship have probably been more important still. Christian worship through the centuries has taken a wide variety of forms, from the spontaneous outpourings of camp meetings and speaking in tongues to the ancient and ornate ceremonial of the Orthodox liturgy. All churches develop over the course of time a "liturgy"—an expected order of words and actions for worship. Members of even the freest tradition would not expect to begin with a sermon and continue on to prayer and hymns, or to hear a sermon before rather than after a reading from scripture. Certain arrangements of the elements of worship become expected because they are logical or traditional. These orders change only slowly and such change is often fiercely resisted.

The Lutheran and Episcopal churches are commonly spoken of as "liturgical churches," by which we mean that their worship follows specific patterns developed through two thousand years of history. They, in common with the Roman Catholic Church, are part of a liturgical tradition that developed within western European culture and helped to shape it. Both Lutherans and Episcopalians can expect that on most Sundays the service will follow the same familiar and predictable order. The prayers and hymns and readings will almost always come from books authorized by the church for the use of its member congregations. Few congregations stray very far from what their denomination's books provide. One sign of our fundamental unity is that the two books used today, the Episcopal *Book of Common Prayer* and the *Lutheran Book of Worship,* are drawn from the same ancient Christian sources.

The Reformation Background

At the time of the Reformation in the sixteenth century virtually all western Christians were accustomed to attending the mass—a eucharistic celebration that was said or sung in Latin by the clergy with minimal involvement of the laity. Lay people participated in the mass by saying private prayers of devotion quietly in their places while the priest recited the words and prayers of the liturgy at the altar in Latin—a language which by this time very few lay people could understand. When the priest held up the wafer at the moment of consecration the people would look up in adoration, but communion was received only on rare occasions and then only the bread, not the wine.

It was not always so. For the early church the eucharistic celebration was a joyful gathering of Christians who came together to give thanks for the death and resurrection of Jesus their Savior and to receive the bread and wine in which he came to be present with them. Through the long centuries of the Middle Ages, that understanding of the eucharist had grown dim. By the time of Luther and Cranmer, the corporate and joyful nature of Christian worship had been largely replaced by a dutiful and even fearful obedience. Instead of gathering in joyful thanksgiving for Christ's death and resurrection, Christians came to seek forgiveness of their sins from the Christ who had become primarily a judge.

In addition, the laity had been so thoroughly excluded from real participation in the church's life and liturgy that in many places priests and monks alone were spoken of as "the church." Even in nineteenth-century England, long after the Reformation, someone being ordained was spoken of as "going into the church," as if lay people were not really members of the Body of Christ.

For well over a century before the Reformation, a number of Christians had begun to feel that Christian worship was in need of renewal. In fourteenth-century England, John Wycliffe had translated the Bible into English and called for an end to clerical abuses. Jan Hus in Prague at the end of the same century had led a movement to restore the right of lay people to receive both the bread and the wine in the Holy Eucharist. Hus and others had also called for the use of the vernacular—the common language used by the people—in worship in place of Latin. The ideas of these and other early reformers provided a background to the work of Luther and Cranmer and others who set out in the sixteenth century to provide reformed patterns of worship as part of a wider reworking of the church's life. Their goal was to build on a deeper knowledge of the Bible (which was by then widely available in a language accessible to the people) and the active participation of the laity in worship as central to the church's life.

While a growing number of Christians in the sixteenth century sensed that something was amiss with the way worship was being offered in their congregations, they had little knowledge of the history of the liturgy or the way it had developed from the church's early days. They also had never had any direct exposure to the liturgical expressions of the Orthodox churches of the east that were so different from those of the west. Their whole experience of worship was shaped by the western medieval pattern that came to obscure the true nature of Christian liturgy. These reform-minded Christians understood that the liturgy was not a mechanical, even superstitious repetition of hidden, semi-magical acts done by the priest on behalf of a largely passive congregation. They shared a common belief that the service needed to be in the language of the people, that they should be encouraged to receive communion frequently, and that they should be able to receive the wine as well as the bread; however, the reformers were deeply divided among themselves over the meaning of the eucharist and the way in which the services needed to be changed to reflect a truer understanding of its nature and purpose.

Fortunately, under the circumstances, both Martin Luther and Thomas Cranmer were cautious and conservative in their approach. They did not entirely eliminate the ancient liturgies, as the more radical reformers did. They recognized that in spite of the corruption of the church's life and worship, the Spirit was still at work among the people of God. Thus they believed it was change within a continuing tradition that was needed, not a wholesale replacement of liturgical patterns that, however corrupt, were nonetheless a central part of people's lives. The problem was not the complete *absence* of the gospel, but the way that gospel had been encrusted with distracting customs and unnecessary requirements. The treasure was still there in earthen vessels, though the earthen vessels had become, perhaps, the focus of more attention than the treasure.

Although Luther and Cranmer were influential in the development of the Lutheran and Anglican traditions, those traditions have, of course, been shaped by many other voices and social forces since the time of the Reformation. Both traditions have lived through many variations of worship styles, and their members have held a wide variety of perspectives on the practice and function of corporate worship. Lutherans and Anglicans have seen times of clergy domination, infrequent celebration of the Lord's Supper, and lax attention to historic patterns of liturgy. Both have experienced periods of emotional and subjective worship as well as dry and rational services. It is remarkable that now, at the beginning of the twenty-first century, these two traditions have converged in so many ways in their approaches to and practice of liturgical worship.

The Lutheran Liturgical Tradition
As the Lutheran tradition spread beyond the various states of Germany to the surrounding countries of central Europe, Scandinavia, and beyond there was no way to impose a single, common liturgy, had such a liturgy even been desired. Instead, a flexible approach

to worship was used to communicate central doctrinal teaching in a variety of cultures and languages. Indeed, a commitment to "evangelical freedom," which was one of Luther's pervasive themes, was also applied to worship and created a certain suspicion of liturgical uniformity. As a result, Lutheran worship has always been characterized by wide variety. On the one hand, many congregations retained a number of ancient practices, even continuing the use of Latin in some places well into the nineteenth century. On the other hand, Lutherans were allowed such a measure of freedom that in some times and places traditional liturgies were abandoned entirely.

That diversity was especially felt as Lutherans in America struggled to maintain their identity or find a new one. Lutherans in America came from a variety of European backgrounds—none of them English. In many areas, therefore, the Lutheran churches served as havens in which immigrants from Europe could find familiar language and customs in an unfamiliar new world. Norwegian, Swedish, Danish, and German were preserved as the languages of worship, instruction, and social gatherings. In the earliest days, clergy were brought from the countries of origin to serve these congregations and to help them preserve their ethnic identity through the church. As time went on, seminaries began to produce leaders on North American soil, but, lacking a unified worship tradition, each group of Lutherans was left to decide for itself whether to import a European liturgy in its inherited language, or to develop one that was more "American" in style and content. These early experiments sometimes had unfortunate results. The classic textbook *The Lutheran Liturgy* written by Luther Reed in 1947 speaks of the "cheap sentiment and bombastic phrases" of some of these early compilations, which were probably characteristic of the times. Lutheran liturgists also felt free to borrow from other traditions, especially *The Book of Common Prayer,* as conditions warranted. In America, as in Europe, efforts were sometimes made to produce a common liturgy for Lutherans and Christians of the Reformed tradition. The growing interest in liturgy in the nineteenth century led many Lutherans to look back to their roots, and by 1868 the General Council had produced a liturgy in English that restored some of the liturgical practices and forms that had fallen into disuse under the influence of rationalism and pietism.

By the early years of the twentieth century North American Lutherans began to desire a greater unity. Part of this deeper concern for Lutheran unity grew out of the slow decline in immigration rates and the fact that the descendants of earlier immigrants were beginning to feel at home here. English was becoming, for most Lutherans, either a first, or at least a common language. The First World War created a new feeling of American ascendancy at the same time that some German-Americans were distancing themselves from ties to the homeland. In addition, there was renewed interest in the roots of the Lutheran movement because of the four-hundredth anniversary of the posting of Luther's Ninety-Five Theses. The production of an English-language liturgy in 1868, *The Church Book,* led to the publication in 1888 of The Common Service. The experience of a common pattern of worship, in turn, further deepened the growing sense of Lutheran unity. All of these factors led naturally to the merger, in November of 1917, of three Lutheran bodies into the United Lutheran Church in America (ULCA). At the same time a more complete work was introduced, *The Common Service Book,* that included occasional services and musical settings for the liturgy, as well as a collection of hymns. These events signal the beginning of a century-long process of Lutheran unification and, in the second half of the century, an increasing passion for ecumenical reunion. They also reflected the development of a formal, standardized liturgy that was both authentically Lutheran and truly American.

In the decades that followed, members of eight distinct Lutheran denominations, including Germans, Swedes, Danes, Finns, and Norwegians, worked together on a project that bore fruit in the late 1950s with the production of a new worship resource, the *Service Book and Hymnal.* This book, known informally as "the red book," was a refinement of the liturgical pattern in the *Common Service Book* and gave further impetus to the movement toward unity. In 1962, after only five years of using the same liturgy, two new national Lutheran bodies were formed: the American Lutheran Church (ALC), and the Lutheran Church in America (LCA). The Lutheran Church-Missouri Synod remained outside these mergers, but joined in the use of this classic American Lutheran worship book. It was the standard for most Lutheran worship in Canada and the United States from 1958 until the publication of the *Lutheran Book of Worship* ("the green book") in 1978. This book, which remains the standard guide for worship in the ELCA, was intended to be ecumenical in the broadest sense: to unite Lutherans, in the short term, but also to affirm the common heritage of Lutherans and other Christians by reclaiming the language of ancient liturgies.

More recently, Lutherans have acquired an alternative service book containing hymns and liturgical forms that offer further possibilities for the enrichment of church services. The use of none of these books, it must be emphasized, is required. Pastors and congregations are free to use them or not, and to alter them in any way. There are Lutheran churches whose worship is completely free and non-liturgical, and others whose services are almost indistinguishable from those of neighboring Episcopal or Roman Catholic churches. Nonetheless, the dominant trend among Lutheran churches in recent years has been toward the recovery of traditional liturgical forms and a recentering of worship in the eucharistic liturgy.

Anglicanism and The Book of Common Prayer

As we have already noted, the Anglican (and therefore Episcopal) sense of the unifying nature of liturgy is part and parcel of its identity. Anglicans have always assumed that all church members would use a single book as a basis for common worship. This assumption grows out of the fact that, unlike the Lutheran experience, *The Book of Common Prayer* was established by the English government for one nation, speaking one language, and was specifically intended as a unifying force. The use of that book would not only regulate worship, but would help unite the people of the British Isles—even those still speaking Cornish, Welsh, or Gaelic—under English language and leadership. That tradition of one book used by all was carried from England to daughter churches founded by Anglicans throughout the world. Having a common prayer book has helped not only to preserve the unity of these new congregations within their own countries, but also to produce a sense of common life in what is now a world-wide communion of churches.

The Anglican insistence on one book did not, however, prevent that book from being used in a wide variety of ways. Although a traditionally elaborate liturgy was retained in some places well into the seventeenth century, with vestments such as copes and chasubles

and the use of incense, the rise of rationalism at the
end of that century led to the virtual abandonment of
the ancient ceremonies focused on the sacraments in
favor of a style of worship centered on scripture and
reason. On Sunday mornings church members no
longer went to the service for the Holy Eucharist, but
instead would find the reading of Morning Prayer,
including the Litany and the first part of the eucharistic service, followed by a lengthy sermon. Some
Episcopalians today still worship in the many surviving colonial church buildings dominated by "three-
decker pulpits" designed to allow a lay clerk on the
lower deck to lead the congregational responses while
the clergyman read the prayer book service from the
second level until he climbed to the top to preach the
sermon. A small communion table was set in front of
the pulpit for those infrequent times, perhaps only
three occasions each year—Christmas, Easter, and
Pentecost—when the Lord's Supper was celebrated.

This pattern of worship was in its turn gradually
superceded in the nineteenth century under the influence of the Gothic revival and the Oxford Movement,
which sought to restore many of the "high church"
practices of the late Middle Ages, and emphasized the
importance of the eucharist and other sacraments. As
more and more Anglicans began to think that the
medieval cathedral in fact provided the best environment for worship, every parish church began to feel
the need for a divided choir, a high altar, and a bishop's chair. Amid bitter controversy, medieval vestments were restored to use and some churches even
reinstituted such pre-Reformation practices as non-
communicating masses (in which only the priest
received the elements) and communion in one kind
(the bread alone) for the laity. At the same time, however, a number of "low church" parishes maintained

the simplicity of their worship and focus on the Word, refusing even to place candles or crosses on what they (and the prayer book) called the Lord's Table. The same *Book of Common Prayer* was used in all these churches, but the divergence of practice spanned an extraordinarily wide range and reflected deep theological differences between the "evangelical" and "catholic" parties.

More recently, the same reliance on a single book that has preserved the church's unity in spite of deep theological and liturgical differences was the source of discord when the church made significant changes in the prayer book revision of 1979. The 1979 *Book of Common Prayer* marked significant changes in worship in the Episcopal Church. For the first time since the Reformation, the liturgy was in contemporary English. The new and revised liturgies also reflected a theological shift in emphasis, from a preoccupation with sin and penitence to a joyful proclamation of God's redeeming love and care for all people. Coming almost simultaneously with the ordination of women, the changes proved too much for some who had thought that the Episcopal Church was defined by Cranmer's language and theological outlook. Although the changes were accepted without much difficulty in many places, they were adopted slowly and reluctantly in some parishes and rejected entirely in a few. Some congregations and individuals went so far as to leave the Episcopal Church to form new churches in which the 1928 prayer book would continue to be used and women would not be ordained.

As the Episcopal Church enters the twenty-first century, the revised *Book of Common Prayer* has won widespread acceptance and produced perhaps the greatest unity in liturgy that the church has ever known. Lay participation in the liturgy has certainly reached new heights, and ancient practices have been revived almost everywhere. In recent years new calls for revision have been made, however, centered largely on the language used and the amount of diversity that is appopriated in the Anglican worship. The fact that the 1979 *Book of Common Prayer* encourages a variety of liturgical practices by providing two forms for most services—one in Elizabethan language and one in contemporary language—and several different forms for the prayer of consecration and the intercessory prayers has led to greater freedom in worship within Anglican churches. Those who desire to use alternative liturgies have also raised the question of whether a single prayer book is still either necessary or possible. For many, the use of masculine pronouns for God and words like "Lord" that imply a masculine deity have become offensive to some, while these words remain familiar and beloved by others. The widespread use of computers and desktop publishing has also made it possible for every parish to produce its own orders of service week by week, and to insert such changes as the priest considers appropriate. The future of prayer book revision is thus somewhat unclear, but since its earliest beginnings *The Book of Common Prayer* has been both a source of unity and a center of controversy, and so far few Episcopalians have been prepared to imagine a church without it.

The Holy Eucharist
The first Christians met together to celebrate the eucharist as Jesus had commanded because Christ was "made known to them in the breaking of the bread" (Luke 24:35). *How* he was present with them was not a question they asked; they knew he was and that was enough. The eucharist was also a celebration of their unity in Christ. An early prayer preserved in the

Episcopal hymnal compares the gathering of Christians into one with the making of one loaf of bread out of scattered grain:

> Watch o'er thy Church, O Lord, in mercy,
> save it from evil, guard it still,
> perfect it in thy love, unite it,
> cleansed and conformed unto thy will.
> As grain, once scattered on the hillsides,
> was in this broken bread made one,
> so from all lands thy Church be gathered
> into thy kingdom by thy Son.

This experience of the presence of Christ in union with others in the church led to worship that was filled with thanksgiving and joy. That understanding of worship changed, however, as the church grew and its position in society was altered. New questions began to be asked about the meaning of Christian worship, and sometimes the answers that were given created new divisions.

In the course of the Middle Ages, as a new European civilization arose out of the ashes of the Roman Empire, the great philosophers of ancient Greece were rediscovered by Christian theologians who attempted to make use of the philosophical systems of Plato and Aristotle to interpret the Christian faith. Plato and Aristotle had been much concerned with the fundamental nature of reality, and Christian theologians began to use their terminology to explain what happens when bread and wine are given to communicants as the body and blood of Christ. There is, they taught, an inner substance of every material thing which constitutes its essential being. Tables may be long or short, red or green, square or round, but all of them have an inner substance which is the same for all tables. So, in the altar bread, theologians decided, the inner, invisible substance is what becomes the body of Christ.

Having determined *what* happens in the eucharist, the theologians moved on to speculate about *when* the change happens. They focused their attention on the "words of institution" spoken by the priest during the eucharistic prayer of the mass, the biblical words reciting what Jesus said and did at the last supper. Jesus had said, "This is my body" (Luke 22:19), and in the liturgy the priest said the same words in Latin: *"Hoc est corpus meum."* These words, then, took on an almost magical importance—indeed, our phrase "hocus pocus" is derived from them. When these words were said, the priest held up the bread while an acolyte rang a bell and communicants looked upward to see the miracle and adore.

Modern liturgical scholars prefer to avoid giving such exclusive weight to the "words of institution" and to think of Christ's coming to be present with us in the elements through the whole action of the liturgy, in the words and actions of the entire assembled congregation, not of the priest or pastor alone. They understand that the four actions of Jesus at the last supper in taking, blessing, breaking, and giving the bread and wine are not reflected narrowly in the words spoken at the last supper, but in the whole liturgical action. The offertory procession, in which members of the congregation bring the elements to the altar, draws attention to the *taking* of the bread and wine; the whole eucharistic prayer is understood to be a giving of thanks or *blessing;* the *breaking* of the bread has its own place in the service immediately following the eucharistic prayer; and the *giving* is, of course, the receiving of communion. Modern scholars would also call attention to the importance attached by the eastern church to the invocation of the Holy Spirit, an aspect missing entirely from the medieval mass but recovered in most western liturgies today.

Luther and Cranmer were uncomfortable with the medieval concentration on a magic moment and a single person but, having no alternative understanding readily available, they remained deeply influenced by it themselves. They thought they were recovering a biblical pattern when they ended the eucharistic prayer with the words of institution. As the priest or pastor said those words, he was to take up the bread and cup, break the bread, and immediately give people communion. The result, however, was to focus attention still on the words of institution and to make of the communion service a simple repetition of the last supper, rather than a thanksgiving for the whole of Christ's life and an anticipation of the end of time and the heavenly banquet, as it was in the early church.

The 1662 English *Book of Common Prayer,* which remains the standard prayer book of the Church of England, still reflects this medieval pattern for the eucharist, and the same pattern is still provided as an alternative in the Lutheran service book. Thus generations of Lutherans and Episcopalians alike have grown up with an understanding of the eucharist somewhat out of focus and shaped by medieval theology because the reformers did not have access to the liturgical sources from the early church that would allow them to break free from their own heritage.

In the same way, because he had grown up with a Christian theology dominated by Greek philosophy and medieval theology, Luther had difficulty finding adequate language with which to explain his beliefs about the eucharist theologically. He believed Christ to be truly present "in, with, and under the bread and wine." The Swiss reformer Ulrich Zwingli, on the other hand, taught that Christ was not in fact present;

the eucharist was simply a "memorial" meal intended only to stimulate the faith of participants. Such a view found expression briefly in the 1552 version of *The Book of Common Prayer,* when Cranmer's first prayer book of 1549 failed to satisfy the more extreme elements of the English reform party. In the first prayer book, the priest giving communion was to say, "The Body of our Lord Jesus Christ, which was given for thee...." Three years later the priest was to say, "Take and eat this in remembrance that Christ died for thee, and feed on him in thy heart by faith...." When Elizabeth I came to the throne, the two sentences were combined into one and that version, which was adopted by the Episcopal Church after the American Revolution in its first prayer book, remains an option even in the 1979 revision.

The combined sentence does, indeed, allow for a range of interpretation and has enabled church members of widely differing views to feel comfortable with a common liturgy. Lutherans, whose liturgy has never qualified the phrase "The Body of Christ given for you," have been surprised to find Zwinglian language enshrined in the Episcopal prayer book and have asked whether Episcopalians do truly believe Christ to be present in the sacrament.

In his effort to restore a biblical pattern to the eucharistic liturgy, Luther swept away the services that had grown up in the Middle Ages around the adoration of the sacrament. Although medieval Christians had not been allowed to receive communion regularly, they had been encouraged to adore Christ present in the sacramental elements, which were kept enshrined in tabernacles on the altar, carried through the streets in solemn processions, and held up in blessing during services of Benediction. Luther was sure this was not the purpose for which the eucharist was instituted and, to avoid such practices among his followers, the bread and wine used in the eucharist were not to be reserved when the service was over. They were consecrated in order to be received, and when that purpose had been served, what was left over no longer had a special nature. It would not be placed in a tabernacle for adoration or future use. Just as some of the words Episcopalians use in the prayer book raise questions for Lutherans, so some Lutheran actions raise questions for Episcopalians. If, as sometimes still happens today, the remaining wine is put back in the bottle at the end of the service to be used again at the next service, Episcopalians sometimes wonder whether Lutherans really believe that Christ is present in the elements.

Lutherans know what they believe because they have expressed it in their theology. Episcopalians know what they believe because they have expressed it in the actions of the liturgy. Both come to think as they do because of a long history that makes it difficult for them to understand another way of saying (or doing) the same thing. Anglicans, being less dependent on theology than Lutherans, have been quite willing to accept the limits of language and the inability of human words to cope with divine mystery. Queen Elizabeth I, for example, is said to have swept aside theological debate over the eucharist with a simple rhyme:

> He was the Word that spake it;
> He took the bread and brake it;
> And what his word did make it,
> That I believe and take it.

Jeremy Taylor, in the middle of the seventeenth century, made the same essential point in different words:

We may in this mystery to them that curiously ask what or how it is (respond), *Mysterium est.* "It is a sacrament, and a mystery"; by sensible instruments it consigns spiritual graces; by the creatures it brings us to'God; by the body it ministers to the spirit.

In the early church, he argued, "many of the fathers laid their hands upon their mouths, and revered the mystery."

That recognition of mystery is important, but Taylor never intended it to be used as an excuse for avoiding theology. Mystery is a vital element in eucharistic theology, but not a substitute for the use of human reason—reason is, after all, a central aspect of the Anglican approach to understanding. The long continued use of well-chosen words gives them a double value. Words explain and speak to reason, but beautiful language carries us beyond the limits of language into the mystery at the heart of our existence. Both are a vital part of the Episcopal approach to worship.

Daily and Occasional Services

The Holy Eucharist is *the* distinctive act of Christian worship, and it is gradually regaining that central place not only in the Lutheran and Episcopal churches, but in other churches as well. But prayer is not limited to the celebration of the eucharist, and over the centuries various services for daily prayer and the celebration of particular occasions in the church's life and those of its members have emerged. Early in the Middle Ages the monastic orders developed a pattern of prayer services held seven times a day that provided an opportunity for further meditation on the psalms and other passages of scripture. Although lay people had little opportunity to take part in these services, these daily offices were an important legacy to the reformers, who hoped to revive them and use them as a means to open the scriptures more fully to clergy and laity alike. However, events following the Reformation led Lutherans and Anglicans in directions rather different from those Cranmer and Luther had anticipated.

Archbishop Cranmer, in England, saw the monastic offices as a cornerstone in his plan to restore a knowledge of the Bible to the laity. Combining the seven monastic offices into two services, one for the morning and one for the evening, he constructed patterns of prayer centered on the Bible that became a vital part of Anglican experience. The 1549 *Book of Common Prayer* begins with tables to show how the Old Testament is to be read through once every year "except certain bokes and Chapiters which bee least edifying," and the New Testament three times except the Apocrypha. The liturgies for Morning Prayer and Evening Prayer set this reading of the scriptures in a context of prayer. It became the boast of the Church of England and the Episcopal Church that the faithful use of the prayer book would make Anglicans more familiar with scripture than the members of any other church.

Most lay people, of course, could not attend church twice a day, but clergy were ordered to read the daily offices and ring the church bell before doing so. Lay people could, however, attend on Sunday, and when the eucharist began to be celebrated less often, Sunday Morning Prayer (or Mattins) and Sunday Evening Prayer (or Evensong) gradually became the chief services. Well into the twentieth century, the familiar order of Sunday services for Episcopalians was 8 A.M. Holy Communion and 11 A.M. Morning Prayer, except on the first Sunday of the month, when the eucharist was celebrated at both services. The canticles and psalms were usually sung to Anglican chant. To this day the service of Evensong, sung in the great cathedrals of England with a choir of men and boys (and often girls in recent years), is very popular. The daily offices had the additional advantage that they could be conducted by lay people. Small country parishes, unable to afford a full-time priest, could still have regular services conducted by a lay person, and families could say Evening Prayer together at the end of the day.

Although Cranmer's daily offices were based in part on German models, the Lutheran reformers never provided liturgies for the daily offices that gained widespread popularity. Large parts of the daily services continued to be said in Latin, and within a century the offices had almost completely disappeared. Beginning in the latter part of the nineteenth century, an effort was made to restore the services of Matins and Vespers, but lacking the long tradition of Anglicanism, the services have not been often used. As a result, when the habit of receiving communion regularly declined in the Lutheran churches, there was no popular service to take the place of the eucharist. On Sundays when communion is not offered, therefore, Lutherans ordinarily simply use the first part of the liturgy for the Eucharist—the service of the Word—with a sermon and hymns.

In addition to daily prayer, there are also special occasions that call for a response of worship. Liturgies for baptisms, weddings, and funerals are provided in the standard prayer book of each church, but Lutherans and Episcopalians have been liberal in providing services to meet all sorts of situations. Cranmer's *Book of Common Prayer* was intended to provide liturgies for every occasion so that no other book would be needed, but from the beginning other books and booklets have appeared on the scene. The primary compilation for Episcopalians today is *The Book of Occasional Services,* which contains at least a dozen additional orders of service, from Advent lessons and carols to vigils for various festivals to the blessing of a pregnant woman, as well as dozens of prayers, blessings, and other resources to enhance services on special occasions. Lutherans have a similar book, *Occasional Services,* with materials for a time of separation or divorce, the retirement of a debt, guidelines for ringing church bells, and many other occasions. The Lutheran book also includes some services—such as those for anointing the sick and for the ordination of pastors—that Episcopalians include in *The Book of Common Prayer* itself.

Music in the Liturgy

Christians have always sung in their worship, and St. Paul himself commended singing to the early church in his letters. Lutherans and Episcopalians have different but equally strong traditions of church music. Luther himself wrote some thirty-seven hymns, of which seven are in the latest Episcopal hymnal, and even Roman Catholics sing his greatest hymn, "A Mighty Fortress is our God." Likewise, the first *Book of Common Prayer* provides instruction for the chanting of lessons, including the epistle and gospel: they are to be sung "in a playne tune after the maner of distinct reading."

The amount and style of singing in Episcopal liturgies have varied widely over time—sometimes with a fair amount of controversy. Although Anglican chant was developed specifically for use at Morning and Evening Prayer, some have preferred to use metrical psalms while others have maintained the ancient plainsong tradition. As for singing of parts of the prayers of the eucharist, some Episcopalians have objected to the practice as "Roman Catholic" and no one setting has ever been adopted. It surprises Episcopalians, therefore, to find that Lutherans include the music of the eucharist in the text of the service and hand out inserts for the Sunday morning bulletin that include the music for the appointed psalm. Indeed, Lutherans have completely integrated their music into the liturgy by making one book for the services, service music, and hymns. Even so, Episcopalians and Lutherans have a majority of their hymn texts and tunes in common; neither would experience much that was unfamiliar in the music of the other tradition.

The Feast to Come
During the course of the twentieth century, a renewed interest in the history and purpose of the liturgy in most major churches led to a growing ecumenical consensus as to the origins of Christian eucharist and the best ways to shape the liturgy for contemporary use. Not only Lutherans and Episcopalians, but Roman Catholics, Congregationalists, Methodists, and Presbyterians, now study the same texts and shape their liturgies with the same goals in mind.

The question asked by both Luther and Cranmer was "What did the ancient church do?" That remains an important question, but today we have more infor-mation and can give more complete answers. Our visually oriented society also has overcome traditional prejudices against color and ceremony that once seemed "too Roman." Liturgical practices such as the keeping of the church year, the use of ashes on Ash Wednesday, the carrying of palms on Palm Sunday, the procession of vested choirs, and the use of candles and crosses on the altar have spread into churches once thought of as non-liturgical. The recent document "Baptism, Eucharist, and Ministry," produced by the World Council of Churches in 1982, sums up a growing convergence among its member churches. More and more, Christians are coming to value the liturgy as the focus of their common life. As we meet each other in Christ's presence and share the life we are offered there, we may come closer to becoming what we are called to be: God's people, the Body of Christ, finding in a shared meal a "foretaste of the feast to come" (*Lutheran Book of Worship*, 66).

For Reflection

What aspect of your denomination's worship life is most important to you?

What has been your experience when worshiping in churches from other denominations? What drew you into the worship experience or what made it uncomfortable for you?

CHAPTER FOUR

GOVERNING OUR CHURCHES

Administration, Organization, and Authority

At the time of the Reformation issues of theology and church government were inseparable. For most Christians, the power of the pope and the way the church was governed influenced and interpreted in very important ways what the church taught. Democracy was a largely unknown concept in the sixteenth century, but long-standing protests over the corrupt use of power and the rising spirit of nationalism gave a special focus to popular discontent. To resist the papacy was to give expression to German, English, and Scandinavian loyalties. Once papal control was ended, the churches of the Reformation were

free to develop new types of government. The intention of the reformers was to create forms that were
more faithful to biblical models and the life of the
early church, but the fact that they were German and
English patterns may have been just as important to
ordinary Christians.

Church government (or "polity," as it is often
called) is the way in which an organization is struc-
tured. It has to do with who makes decisions, how people are chosen for various roles, and where authority
and responsibility are placed. Over the centuries the
church has developed a variety of structures to carry
on its mission and administer its inner life. Like any
other organization or institution, Christian polity is
not static; it has changed often in the past and continues to be refined and adjusted today to meet changing
circumstances. Churches borrow freely from secular
sources when appropriate and create new forms of
governance when necessary, yet they always seek to
build on biblical models and traditional patterns that
have stood the test of time.

It is important to bear in mind that ordained ministry and church government are not the same thing.
Bishops in Britain's early Celtic church had no role in
church government; the church was administered by
the abbots of the various monasteries, while bishops
had only a sacramental role. Especially since the time
of the Reformation, some Christians have imagined a
church in which lay leaders govern while clergy con-
fine themselves to ministries of preaching, teaching,
sacraments, and pastoral care. Traditionally bishops
have filled both administrative and pastoral roles, with
the balance shifting radically in various times and
places.

Unlike institutions of purely human origin, the
church always sees Jesus Christ as its supreme head.

He is known as our High Priest, our Good Shepherd, our Lord, and the Guardian of our Souls. Every form of Christian polity is an attempt to be faithful to the intention of Christ, and to be obedient to Christ's will and purpose. Thus every form of church government is intended to serve our common mission to preach the Word, administer the sacraments, forgive sins, and serve our neighbors in obedience to our Lord's commands.

While all Christians probably agree with the above generalities, they most emphatically do not agree on their implications. As early as the second century, the nearly universal pattern of church polity seems to have included regional overseers called bishops, local overseers called presbyters, and an order of assisting ministers called deacons. As the church grew in numbers, expanded geographically, and had to deal with an increasingly diverse membership, the structure became more elaborate. The threat of heresies required the church to find a way to define orthodox beliefs and safeguard the apostolic tradition. As the church emerged from the long years of persecution and adjusted to the new reality of official status in the Roman Empire in the fourth century, it began to create an elaborate structure of archbishops, bishops, priests, archdeacons, deacons, subdeacons, and a variety of lay orders. Authority and responsibility were conferred on those holding office with a prayer invoking the gifts of the Holy Spirit and the laying on of hands. Meetings of bishops and theologians representing all the various churches in the east and west, known as the ecumenical councils, were convened from the fourth to the eighth centuries to discuss and clarify questions of doctrine and practice within the church.

One of the most frustrating stumbling blocks to greater Christian unity today is our disagreement over the ancient pattern of church government. For many Christians, the early structure is an integral part of the apostolic faith. It is its safeguard and its divinely ordered form, and any major alteration signals a departure from the revealed pattern of church life. Without this order, it is feared, local communities will easily go astray, losing their connection to each other and to the foundational traditions of the Christian faith. For others, the highly organized and formal hierarchy of ordained leaders represents an offensive attempt to wrest power and authority from Christ and replace it with human rulers, thus stifling the freedom of the Holy Spirit to raise up charismatic ministries. To them this ordering of ministries appears to be a centralizing of power that deprives the local assembly of believers of their rightful and divinely authorized royal priesthood, and an addition to the biblical record that goes well beyond the will of God, distracting Christians from their mission in the world.

Finding a balance among these various perspectives has never been easy. Christians have struggled with such issues from the beginning and still do. Roman Catholics find themselves in conflict over the power of the papacy, while Baptists disagree over their prized congregational autonomy and the amount of power to delegate to a national coordinating structure. So too, Lutherans and Episcopalians find themselves constantly readjusting the roles and authority of bishops, governing councils, and congregations and the ways in which they relate to one another.

Varieties of Church Government
Many different forms of government have been developed in the long history of the Christian church.

Church leaders have been elected by both lay people and clergy and by closed groups of clergy; they have been chosen by the general public and appointed by secular rulers. Some have copied the style of secular rulers, living in palaces and attended by throngs of servants; others have desired a simpler form of communal life in the church, establishing monasteries with their own leaders and rules of life. Over the centuries Christians have often imagined that those of an earlier age lived a life closer to the gospel, and they have tried to reform church structures to recreate something closer to that vision. In the same way, some of the sixteenth-century reformers took radical steps to reject the patterns they inherited and to create new structures of Christian life, while others were content with far less sweeping rearrangements.

The names of some denominations reflect their beliefs about polity. The Presbyterian Church, for example, is named for its system of presbyteries, which are committees of elders ("presbyters") who govern the life of the denomination; this system is also used by the Reformed Church and other churches in the Calvinist or Reformed tradition. The Congregational tradition, on the other hand, is based on the idea that all true authority resides in local assemblies. Cooperation between congregations can occur but is voluntary; there is to be no power vested in any person or office outside the parish. That principle is hard to live out in a world where some issues— like pension funds and publications—cannot easily be administered at the local level. Baptists and Congregationalists alike have felt a need to create national boards to deal with these matters for them. It should be noted that the present United Church of Christ, which is often called Congregationalist, is not truly so. The UCC has groupings of congregations, called associations, that are roughly similar to an Episcopal deanery or a Lutheran conference in size, but have some of the authority of an Episcopal diocese or a Lutheran synod. Indeed, the choosing of a name that has the word "United" in it signified the departure from strict Congregationalism that took place when the former Congregational Church merged with the Evangelical and Reformed Church. There are, however, many independent churches that do practice a strictly congregational style of governance.

Since the word "episcopal" refers to bishops, one might expect to find that the Episcopal Church is governed by bishops. The elaborate vestments Episcopal bishops wear often lead people to assume they have equally impressive power to make decisions, but the vestments and title are misleading. In fact, the Episcopal Church is not governed exclusively by its bishops. Fundamental decisions in the Episcopal Church are made by conventions of clergy and laity, and the ongoing administration of a diocese is governed by the bishop working with a committee of clergy and lay leaders. The Episcopal Church polity actually includes elements of the congregational and presbyterian systems, since congregations have considerable freedom and clergy councils play an important role in diocesan and national affairs.

A more nearly "episcopal" pattern of church government can be found in the Methodist Church, the African Methodist Episcopal Church, and the African Methodist Episcopal Zion Church. The United Methodist Church was, in fact, once known as the Methodist Episcopal Church but changed its name to avoid confusion and to reflect a merging of northern and southern churches after the Civil War and the inclusion of the Evangelical United Brethren in the 1960s. Bishops in these churches (though acting with the advice of district superintendents) can assign clergy and make important decisions that Lutheran and Episcopal bishops cannot make on their own.

The names of other communions (including most Lutheran churches, for example) do not refer to their structure. One exception would be the Church of the Lutheran Brethren, whose name does emphasize the role of the laity in the life of the Body of Christ. The same is true for the United Brethren and the Unitas Fratrum (Unity of the Brethren, commonly known as Moravians). While not explicitly defining their polity, the authority of the laity is affirmed in these denominations, while the authority of the clergy is limited. The point is that polity both shapes and is shaped by a communion's sense of its identity and mission.

In general, the Episcopal Church in the United States of America and the Evangelical Lutheran Church in America have been willing to appreciate and appropriate many of the patterns of early church life. Both have bishops, presbyters (Episcopal priests and Lutheran pastors), deacons, and collegial structures of governance. Both are organized into parishes that serve local communities, ideally each with one or more clergy. The parishes are linked within a wider area overseen by a bishop—an Episcopal diocese and a Lutheran synod. The dioceses and synods are the units that make up the national denomination, with a governing convention, a national staff, and a presiding bishop (with offices in New York for Episcopalians and in Chicago for Lutherans). The national bodies are further linked to worldwide communions—the Anglican Communion and the Lutheran World Federation. These worldwide bodies, however, exist primarily for consultation and not to make decisions that are binding on the national churches. Both the Evangelical Lutheran Church in America and the

Episcopal Church belong to the World Council of Churches which, like our worldwide structures, is not a legislative body but does function to engage many kinds of Christians in conversation about a wide variety of issues of faith and life. Both churches have monastic orders (though there is only one Lutheran monastery in America, while there are many Episcopal communities), but these are voluntary organizations that take no part in church government. While these patterns of church polity are not identical to those found in scripture or the early church, they seek to model themselves on the biblical pattern as nearly as possible. At the same time, they attempt to maintain the balance between connectedness and local freedom, between continuity and adaptability that marked the communities of the New Testament and early church.

Laws, Rules, and Rubrics
The Lutheran Church, holding fast to Luther's belief in "evangelical freedom," has surprisingly few rules and regulations. For one simple example, *The Book of Common Prayer* and *Lutheran Book of Worship* both provide rubrics directing members when to sit, stand, or kneel in the liturgy, but *The Book of Common Prayer* goes on to provide many further directions and guidelines, such as appropriate times of the year for baptism, that the bride stands to the right of the priest and the groom to the left, that one party to a marriage must be baptized, that the coffin must be closed before the funeral service begins, and so on. Older prayer books directed that a white cloth must be placed on the altar and that the bread should be of the best quality. Like Lutherans, Episcopalians value freedom—but they have always given even greater weight to "doing things right."

Beyond the rubrics, Episcopalians have a constitution as well as a set of laws called canons that regulate the organization of parishes and dioceses, outline the requirements of character and education for ordination, provide procedures for the discipline of clergy, and outline requirements for marriage, among many other matters. The Evangelical Lutheran Church in America also has a constitution, but this constitution is all-inclusive; anything not included there is handled through bylaws. The differences between the sets of laws is striking. The constitution and canons of the Episcopal Church provide much more guidance on the duties of parish clergy, while the Lutheran constitution includes a detailed statement of faith. Episcopalians find their statements of faith in *The Book of Common Prayer,* while Lutherans leave the parish clergy a great deal of "evangelical freedom" in carrying out their ministry. Unlike the Episcopal Church, the Evangelical Lutheran Church in America sees itself as a new denomination, a merger of older bodies, feeling its way and reluctant to set more limits than seem absolutely necessary. But all its clergy receive the same guidance through instruction in seminary and letters from the conference of bishops and the bishop of the synod. Some have humorously noted that they also tend—along with many Episcopalians and other Christians—to be guided by seven words that did not come from the cross: "We have always done it that way."

Making Decisions

Both the Episcopal and Evangelical Lutheran churches reflect the democratic process of decision-making that is part of every aspect of American life. For example, both churches use a system of elections with votes cast by both ordained and lay members to choose their

bishops. All the governing structures in both denominations are made up of lay and ordained members
who are chosen in elections. The Evangelical
Lutheran Church in America gives lay people a sixty-
percent voice in its national assembly and attempts to
have equal representation of men and women. The
General Convention of the Episcopal Church consists
of two houses, one of bishops and one with equal
numbers of clergy and lay people, but on important
matters the clergy and lay people vote separately and
no action can be taken without a majority of all three
groups. In neither tradition does any one person or
any small group possess power to set policy, form
practice, or determine matters of faith. Both are governed by constitutions and specific rules that regulate
any changes in the way they live out the faith. The secular but very useful *Robert's Rules of Order* is utilized in
all legislative bodies in both communions.

At the local level, every congregation has a governing board made up of elected laity. The Episcopal
Church calls this body a vestry or mission committee;
the Evangelical Lutheran Church terms it a council.
There are typically between nine and twelve members
of such a group, meeting monthly to oversee the life
of the parish. The canons of the Episcopal Church
limit the vestry's authority to matters of finance and
property and calling a new rector, but most vestries
today have committees on education and worship and
work with the clergy on setting policy for all areas of
parish life. Most congregations own their own buildings and can make decisions about the physical plant
and grounds. Episcopal congregations, however, need
diocesan approval to sell or mortgage property.

Both traditions give authority to congregations to
call their clergy, though in the Episcopal Church the
call is issued by the vestry and in the Lutheran Church

by the congregation as a whole. In both churches, the bishop must concur with the selection. If clergy need to be disciplined, it will be the bishop, or someone from the bishop's staff, who directs and administers the process.

Bishops

While both the Lutheran and Episcopal churches have clergy called bishops, there are some differences between the two churches in relation to the choosing of bishops and the role they play. Episcopalians elect bishops to serve until retirement age or death. Evangelical Lutherans, on the other hand, elect bishops for six-year terms, with no limit on successive terms up to retirement age. Part of the agreement with the Episcopal Church is that Lutheran bishops will now remain bishops for life, although they may resign or retire from their synod position. Both churches select their bishops through a democratic process: Lutheran bishops are elected by the synod assembly and Episcopal bishops by the diocesan convention. The synod assembly is comprised of all the clergy in the synod (including non-parish clergy) and at least two lay people from each congregation; all decisions are made by majority vote. Diocesan conventions include all parochial and non-parochial clergy, and one or more lay delegates from each parish. To be elected a bishop in the Episcopal Church, a candidate must have a majority of both clergy and lay votes.

Since Lutheran bishops (and their predecessors, who were known as superintendents and presidents) have traditionally functioned as administrators, only one bishop is needed in each synod. In recent years, however, Lutherans have seen an increasing emphasis on a pastoral role for the bishop. To help the bishop fill the many tasks of the office, he or she normally chooses assistants, who may be either lay or clergy. The Episcopal Church, on the other hand, has long stressed the role of bishop as "chief pastor," expecting bishops to visit parishes annually and insisting that bishops must be the ones who confirm and receive new members. Therefore larger dioceses often have a need for more than one bishop to carry out these tasks. Titles such as bishop coadjutor, suffragan bishop, assisting bishop, and assistant bishop may be used, depending on the process by which they are chosen and the role they will fill.

Clerical Titles
Some words about titles for other ordained leaders in the Episcopal and Lutheran churches may be appropriate here. In the Episcopal Church, the priest in charge of a self-supporting parish is called the rector. He or she, after being elected, is instituted by the bishop and is given tenure. The parish cannot remove a rector without the bishop's consent but the vestry can request the bishop to intervene if it believes there are grounds for doing so. The title vicar is normally used for the priest in charge of a mission congregation that is financially supported in part by the diocese. Such congregations cannot choose their clergy, though bishops may give them opportunity to make their wishes known. Assisting clergy in larger parishes are given a variety of titles, such as curate and assistant rector.

The Evangelical Lutheran Church in America calls all its clergy pastors. In larger congregations there may be assistant pastors, associate pastors, or even co-pastors. The term vicar may be used sometimes to refer to a seminarian serving as an intern. ELCA pastors may be removed by a two-thirds vote of the congregation. This is an unusual procedure; most pastors serve from the time they are elected until they resign or retire.

What we see in these two church traditions as a whole, therefore, are two very similar expressions of Christian community life. In both the Lutheran and Episcopal churches there is a commitment to the democratic spirit of our age, with a great deal of participation at all levels by as wide a variety of members as is practical. There are mechanisms for accountability and various checks and balances. Issues of faith and practice are debated and studied. At some point, votes are taken and decisions are made by those who have been selected to take particular responsibilities. Yet democracy does not mean the freedom to create new structures or creeds without regard for tradition. Both churches have a deep commitment to retaining ancient patterns and titles that have stood the test of time.

For Reflection
Who governs in your local church? At the regional level? At the national level?

How are your church leaders elected, appointed, selected? Does that process invite you in or keep you out?

If you have served in a governing role in your church, what was that experience like for you? What growth did you experience because of it?

CHAPTER FIVE

A MINISTRY OF OVERSIGHT

The Role of Bishops

The worship and theology of the church have not developed haphazardly over time, but have been cultivated at least in part by those who exercise leadership within the church. One of the most influential leadership positions in the history of the church remains that of bishops. Although bishops have exercised many different roles in the church, their work has usually involved some kind of oversight: our term "bishop" is derived from the Greek word *episcopos,* which means "overseer." Who oversees the church and how they do it has been a controversial issue in the life of the church from the very beginning. In the early church, when questions of authority were raised, bishops argued that because they were personally commissioned by other bishops who came before them in an unbroken chain from the apostles, their authority was also handed down directly from the apostles. This claim of "historic succession" has been central to the identity of Anglicans and has been preserved as well in some Lutheran churches, though not those in the United States.

The importance of historic succession—and of episcopal ministry in general—has long been a matter of debate among Lutherans and Episcopalians. Most recently, it was the main stumbling block for Lutherans in the effort to establish a relationship of full communion with Episcopalians. Some Lutherans have seen the historic succession of episcopal ministry as a useful way to symbolize Christian unity; others have remained reluctant to adopt a symbol that might seem to overshadow the gospel's unifying power, especially after centuries of having preserved the apostolic faith without a uniform practice of historic succession. Episcopalians have also differed among themselves on the weight they would give to historic succession, some claiming it to be the essence of a united church, others holding it to be a useful but not essential symbol of unity. "Episcopacy," noted Austin Farrer, an Anglican priest, theologian, and preacher at Oxford in the middle of the twentieth century, "is a dish we are relentless in forcing on others, though we are unable to digest it ourselves." Certainly it has been true that Episcopalians have tended to insist on episcopacy as a basis for union with other churches, only to discover that they can agree with other Christians on almost everything but that!

Because historic succession has been so hotly debated in recent years, especially in the Lutheran

Church, it is important to have an understanding of the evolution of the role of bishops in the two traditions. We need to look carefully at the various paths taken by different churches in the Reformation era, but also to ask why it is that there has been so much disagreement about an aspect of church life that has endured for nearly two thousand years. Perhaps part of our difficulty is that we have yet to see what a truly apostolic ministry would look like: those who have trouble with episcopacy tend to be put off not by the role as it might be and should be, but by the imperfect models known at the time of the Reformation and those in use today.

The Reformation

If we begin by asking what the episcopate looked like to Christians at the time of the Reformation, we will discover that it was distinctly different from what we see today in any American church. The biggest difference was that bishops, both in Germany and in England, were not simply ministers of the church but also part of the secular government. Some German bishops, in fact, *were* the secular government, serving not only as chief administrator of the regional church but also as the prince who ruled the state. In England, bishops were members of the House of Lords, serving under the king as part of the secular government. English rulers commonly appointed men as bishops who had administrative and diplomatic skills so that they could serve both the church and the state. In fact, they would not even have envisioned a distinction between state and church as we understand it. Thomas Cranmer first came to the attention of Henry VIII as a man who could serve his interests as a diplomat, negotiating with civil and religious leaders in Europe in the matter of the king's marriage. Cranmer's success in that role led to his later appointment as Archbishop of Canterbury. And it should be noticed that it was the king, with the pope's consent, who appointed Cranmer to that position.

Clergy in the Middle Ages were often the only educated people, so it was natural for kings and princes to call on them to serve in what we would call secular as well as religious functions. In addition, there was far less clarity than today about the orders of ministry. Although there had been a strong tradition of a threefold ministry of bishops, priests, and deacons in the church of the early Middle Ages, Pope Innocent III had added a fourth order in 1207 by including subdeacons. The ordering of ministries in the church was further complicated by a profusion of "minor orders" that men passed through on their way to being ordained deacon or priest. The four minor orders (porter, acolyte, reader, and exorcist), when added to the three major orders, provided a neat sevenfold pattern and also gave those so ordained the "benefit of clergy," placing them under the authority of the church rather than the secular courts.

Further obscuring the traditional threefold pattern of ministry were those with higher positions of authority within a certain level of ordained ministry, such as cardinals, archbishops, archdeacons, and popes. Cardinals, in fact, were not necessarily either bishops or priests, since lay people and deacons could serve as cardinals. Similarly, members of monastic orders might be ordained or not, but if they were tonsured (had shaven heads), they were counted as clerics. To complicate matters even more, there were ordained people who served important roles in the state and lay people who played important roles in the church. Under the circumstances, it is more surprising that the Church of England retained and insisted on the threefold pattern of ordination than that Luther set out to clarify the situation by speaking of a single ordained ministry.

Looking back today from an American perspective, the reforms sought by Luther seem simple and obvious. Ministry, he insisted, had to do with obedience to the gospel, and those chosen for the church's ordained ministry should have the consent of those they would serve. Although the issue is still much debated, it seems evident that Luther had no fundamental objection to the title of bishop or to clergy serving in a ministry of supervision, so long as they understood their role to be in service to the gospel. Luther's close associate, Philip Melancthon, wrote: "The cruelty of the bishops is the reason for the abolition of canonical government in some places in spite of our earnest desire to keep it." In Sweden, where the bishops accepted Luther's reforms, the ministry of bishops in historic succession has continued to this day. Thus there seems to be no inherent conflict between Lutheranism and a ministry of bishops in historic succession.

Another reform modern American Christians often associate with the Reformation is the separation of church and state, but there was no obvious reason in the reformers' minds why the church's ministry should be completely separated from secular government. Such a division seemed unnecessary in England once the government had given its support to a reformed church. It seemed perfectly appropriate under the circumstances for the ruler to have authority over the church as well as the civil government and for the church to be established by governmental authority. The king, after all, was simply replacing the pope, who was also, it should be remembered, a ruler with temporal jurisdiction; both the king and the pope combined secular and religious authority in their persons. So, after the Reformation, the king in his religious role would appoint the Archbishop of Canterbury, who in turn would preside at coronations and place the crown on royal heads. Indeed, the leading bishops of the Church of England still serve as members of the House of Lords and are commonly greeted as "My Lord." Likewise, English bishops today are not elected but appointed by the king or queen, and most parish clergy are appointed by individuals or outside authorities such as bishops or colleges or committees that have retained that right from ancient tradition.

In the same way, in Germany the division between areas that remained loyal to Roman authority and those that supported Luther's reforms followed territorial lines, and the allegiance of the ruler determined the faith of the citizens. It seemed perfectly natural to Luther for secular princes who supported him to play the role of bishop in supervising the church in their territories: in the Grand Duchy of Baden, for example, the Grand Duke, though himself a Roman Catholic, served as bishop to both the Lutheran and Reformed congregations in his jurisdiction. Not until the end of World War I and the establishment of a democracy in Germany was a complete break made between church and state. Even today, however, taxes are used in Germany to support the church.

In the eyes of the reformers, bishops and priests were not clergy in different orders but clergy with different functions (as a rector and a curate are today in the Episcopal Church). This distinction in orders of ministry had often been blurred in pre-Reformation theology as well, so it is hardly surprising that the idea of a single order of ministry persisted in the reformed churches, including the Church of England. In Sweden the different titles were retained and the historic episcopate continued, but the Swedes saw bishops and priests as being part of one ministry. The Church of England likewise retained the distinction but did not, at first, insist on it. Richard Hooker, the great theologian of Queen Elizabeth's reign, held that episcopacy should be retained where it was available as "the ordinary institution of God," but that it had and could give way to non-episcopal ordination where episcopal ordination was not available. Many Anglicans continued to hold that opinion and for that reason John Wesley thought it was quite proper for him, as a priest, to ordain clergy to serve as bishops in the Methodist societies of America.

One change that was on the agenda of all the reformed churches was to develop a process for selecting individuals for ordained ministry who were called both inwardly by the Holy Spirit and outwardly by the people they would serve. Those to be ordained were examined publicly as to their sense of vocation. The ordination services created by the reformers continued to recognize civil authority but they also required approval by the people, giving them at least an opportunity to express opposition to the proposed ordination. Ordinations were to be public services, held on Sundays or saints' days so lay people could be present. It was also specified that clergy were to be ordained to a specific ministry in a specific place; they were not simply to be made priests as part of an order without a ministry in a particular parish, institution, or diocese.

The Episcopate in the Episcopal Church

The continued existence of the traditional episcopate in England left its imprint on Anglicans in the New World in a number of ways. In the first place, it meant that they assumed the existence of episcopacy even though they did not possess it. Although several attempts were made to obtain an episcopal ministry for the American colonies, opposition on both sides of the Atlantic prevented any of them from coming to fruition.

This opposition was based on the assumption that episcopacy was part of the secular government. On the English side, it seemed that transplanting episcopacy to the New World would be a step toward American independence, since the colonists would then have one of the necessary ingredients of self-government. Some Americans, on the other hand, worried that the arrival of bishops who were part of the government would be a step toward a stricter imposition of English rule. Those who had fled England to establish an independent style of Christianity were, of course, especially opposed to a New World episcopate, and at the same time Anglicans in the southern colonies who had learned to enjoy a bit of freedom from episcopal authority were also in no hurry to bring bishops any nearer.

As a result, through nearly two hundred years of colonial history, Anglicans in America were dependent on England for whatever episcopal oversight and ministry they experienced. The supply of clergy was entirely dependent on trans-Atlantic travel: Americans who sought ordination had to go to England to obtain it. If more clergy were needed, they had to be imported from England. If colonial Anglicans were to be confirmed, they could only receive that rite in England—and the result was that few were. The prayer book had always required that "none shall be admitted to communion until they be confirmed," but that was modified in 1662 to make an exception for those "ready and desirous to be confirmed," which included most American Anglicans.

The odd mixture of dependence and independence experienced by American Anglicans produced radically different results in the various colonial environments. In the southern colonies, where the church was established, it provided an experience of some degree of self-government and, again, a secularized version of ecclesiastical oversight. Lacking bishops, the governor and the House of Burgesses became the ultimate arbiters of church life. Colonial vestries discovered that they could control parish life by keeping clergy on a short financial string. Southern Anglicans became accustomed to a non-episcopal form of church life and rather liked it. In New England, on the other hand, where Congregationalism was established, Anglicans depended on English mission societies for support and church government remained very much in the hands of the clergy. When the Revolution was over, it was the Anglicans in New England who sent Samuel Seabury to Britain in 1784 for the traditional form of consecration.

The first task of the newly independent American Episcopal Church was to sort out what role bishops would play. Clearly they would no longer have a political role, so for the first time in centuries there would be bishops whose only role was within the church. What would they do within the church? New England Anglicans insisted that bishops would have authority in each diocese and would have a separate house in a national convention. They saw no need for a lay voice anywhere in the church's government. Southern Anglicans, on the other hand, had learned to believe in lay government and were not sure bishops were even necessary; certainly they saw no reason to give them a separate house in the government of the church. For awhile it seemed possible that there would be two very different offspring of the Church of England in the new country, but eventually a compromise was worked out that created a convention in which bishops, clergy, and lay people were all represented but bishops were seated in a separate house.

So the American Episcopal Church acquired bishops, but unfortunately the more important question of what bishops were *for* was not decided. If they were no longer part of the state establishment, what were they? For a while they served simply as rectors of large parishes, called on to preside at conventions and available to confirm or ordain on request. Gradually they gained more authority: a significant role in the training and placing of clergy and the right to remove clergy for serious cause. On the national level, they held a veto power over actions of the clergy and laity. But all this was administrative in nature and could in theory be done equally well by a priest or lay person. Even today the full scope of the episcopate as a ministry in service to the gospel, with the bishop acting as chief pastor of clergy and laity, remains to be fully discovered.

Bishops in the Episcopal Church, as a result of this history, do not have enormous power. Roman Catholic and Methodist bishops, as well as bishops in other parts of the Anglican Communion, have considerably more power to control clergy and parishes. But bishops of the Episcopal Church do have enormous freedom to define their role. Some delegate large parts of the administrative work to clergy and lay assistants, thus freeing themselves to be pastors and teachers. Others believe their administrative and disciplinary role prevents them from being pastors, so they delegate the pastoral care of clergy and parishes to archdeacons or others. Many bishops travel regularly in their dioceses, meeting with clergy and parishioners for Bible study and leading them in mission. Dioceses choosing a new bishop can define their needs in terms of an administrator, pastor, evangelist, spiritual leader, or theologian, and then try to elect someone who fits this description. Thus episcopacy in the experience of American Episcopalians continues to evolve as the church in this country changes and grows.

Lutherans and Episcopacy

What happens if you look to your bishops to oversee your congregations and ordain your new clergy, but they refuse to do so? This was the situation in sixteenth-century Germany. While the German reformers saw themselves as trying to correct "certain abuses," their bishops saw them as stirring up a wholesale rebellion against Christ's Holy Church. Perceiving the reformers to be dangerous schismatics, the bishops refused to support the theologians, clergy, nobility, or congregations who joined the growing chorus for reform. Most important, new clergy could not receive the rite of ordination from the bishops. Both civil and ecclesiastical penalties were levied against the reformers, with the bishops' full approval. It was this state of affairs that set the tone for so much of the rhetoric in Lutheran writings that sounds strongly anti-episcopal.

Lutherans in Germany solved this problem by selecting Christian noblemen to exercise the office of bishop, even though the title could not be used in the traditional sense. If those who held the title refused to carry out their calling, they reasoned, then others who were willing and able would be asked to fulfill the duties of the office without the title. Their loyalty to the gospel would be accepted as a substitute for the pope's blessing as the basis for their status as overseers. For the first Lutherans this was not a rejection of episcopacy as an office, but merely a replacement of negligent, even cruel, bishops with people who would bring to the office the faith and commitment that it required. This tactic was not intended to be a radical break with ancient practice, but an emergency response to a situation in which the individuals who bore the traditional titles were unwilling to embody the ministry of the office. In Sweden, for example, the bishops were sympathetic to the Lutheran reforms, so their office was not redefined or reassigned to others. To this day, the Church of Sweden has maintained the historic episcopate.

The title that was commonly used in the German church for the episcopal office was "superintendent." People with that title saw to it that the local churches had what they needed to carry on their ministries. Ordinations and confirmations were assigned to local clergy, under the supervision of the nobleman who was the superintendent. This arrangement worked well to provide continuity to the church when its official overseers withheld their blessings.

At this stage in the Reformation there was still hope for reconciliation with Rome, though that hope was soon dashed. The Augsburg Confession was not accepted by those loyal to Rome as a formulation of the orthodox faith, as it was intended, but was seen as a rejection of the authority of Rome and, as such, a rejection of the whole Christian tradition. The Council of Trent, which met between 1545 and 1563, was called to refute the stance of the reformers and to establish the dogmas that defined the Roman church. This council made it clear that the German bishops would never reconsider their resistance to ordaining or confirming those who espoused Lutheran ideas. With that development, the emergency provisions became an enduring feature of the Lutheran movement, since it was the German experience, not the Swedish, that was to shape most North American strands of Lutheranism.

Lutherans, along with other reformed bodies, drew further and further away from Roman Catholicism (and, not coincidentally, from each other). They became institutionalized denominations, each with its own unique culture of piety and practice that was increasingly less influenced by other Christian traditions. By the eighteenth century bloodshed had ceased, but suspicions and stereotypes remained. Even into the twentieth century one of the most damning charges that could be made against a proposed change in liturgy, vestments, or eucharistic practice was that it was "too catholic." In America the growing fervor for democracy and individualism was absorbed into the Lutheran Church, although most American Christians realized that total congregational independence was not the ideal. Even many of the Christians who espoused a congregational system linked arms with other believers to carry on wider missionary tasks.

Lutherans were not of one mind about the best form for American Lutheranism. The freedom they had discovered through their emergency use of self-appointed leaders was well suited to the climate of American church life. They did not have to depend upon European leaders to choose overseers or provide clergy for new congregations. At the same time, the natural affinities they had for one another led them to experiment with a variety of forms of linking ecclesiastical structures. Sometimes their desire to create an American Lutheran Church was based on language, hymnody, liturgical similarity, or noble inclinations for more effective missionary outreach. Other times there were less high-minded factors, such as mutual distrust of Calvinist, Anabaptist, and Roman Catholic Christians.

Early attempts during the 1700s to develop a Lutheran Ministerium brought areas of both agreement and disagreement quickly to the surface. Two defining aspects of American Lutheranism emerged at that time. The first was that there would be a distinctly *Lutheran* presence in America: Lutherans wanted to carry on the specific heritage of the German and Scandinavian Reformation and did not wish to be melded into a generic American protestantism. The other was that the Lutheran presence in America would not be in the form of a single, unified denomination. Most Lutherans soon came to be organized into groups of congregations called synods, led by leaders who were still called superintendents, or, in some places, presidents. Lay involvement in choosing leaders was a feature of Lutheran structures in America from the beginning. Synods tended to be ethnic and linguistic at first, as Germans, Swedes, Norwegians, Finns, Danes, and immigrants from Slovakia, the Baltic states, and Iceland were inclined to gravitate toward those who shared their mother tongue and culture. Synods would gather in conventions to make decisions about leadership and worship, as well as missionary work. They would also discuss their relationships to other Lutheran synods.

Over time, mostly during the latter half of the nineteenth century, a consensus emerged to seek to unify American Lutherans. By the beginning of the twentieth century there were still dozens of Lutheran bodies, but the groundwork for Lutheran unity had been laid and a series of mergers followed. The United Lutheran Church in America was formed from the General Synod, the General Council, and the General Council South. Though encompassing a variety of traditions, this body had a strong German core and was deeply influenced by the work of Henry

Melchior Muhlenberg during the mid 1700s. Other mergers also followed ethnic lines: the Augustana Synod was a predominantly Swedish body, while the Danish Evangelical Lutheran Church gathered Lutherans from Denmark. The Danish group later merged into the American Lutheran Church in the 1960s. The Suomi Synod, a Finnish body, was formed in 1890. The Lutheran Church-Missouri Synod resulted from a large migration of Germans in the mid 1800s to Missouri and remains to this day a separate strand of Lutheranism.

By the end of the nineteenth century, the English language was in wider use in worship books and Sunday services, though European languages still dominated much confirmation instruction. A resurgence of Lutheran scholarship in the early twentieth century and the celebration of various milestones in the Lutheran Reformation prompted renewed zeal to express Lutheranism in North America in a way that was more unified and faithful to the original reformers' vision, while at the same time encouraging a true American church, not just a vestige of immigration. This movement led to the completion of two large mergers in the early 1960s. One created the American Lutheran Church (ALC), the other the Lutheran Church in America (LCA), both names reflecting the desire to be both American and Lutheran at the same time. Only the Lutheran Church-Missouri Synod and several smaller, stricter bodies refrained from this movement toward Lutheran unity.

At the time of the two large mergers, the title for the overseers was president. Elections were democratic in nature and presidents held office for a set term of years. The structure of national church offices was based on a corporate model, with boards, commissions, and bureaus to carry on the work of the wider church. Synods were often large, so that it was not possible for a synod president to be a source of pastoral care for the clergy or congregations within his (at that time only men could be ordained, so all presidents were male) responsibility. This is not to say that some presidents were not pastoral in style, but rather that the size and structure of the church did not allow the kind of close pastoral relationship that was possible in an age when each city had a bishop.

During the 1970s, there emerged among Lutherans a renewed desire to have church leaders who would exercise the office of Word and Sacraments instead of being primarily administrators. Presidents were required to be ordained pastors, but were being asked to function as executive directors of corporations. The hunger for pastoral leadership led to a change in name as well as focus: presidents again became bishops, and the church began to call forth the pastoral gifts of those chosen for the office. It should be noted, however, that the recovery of even the title "bishop" raised objections within some circles of Lutheranism. Fears of concentrated power, presumption to special status, or a drifting toward Rome were unsettling to a number of church members. Looking back, we can see that not much changed except the title. Some bishops continued to be very efficient executives, while others were more pastoral in their style of leadership. At the same time, the Lutheran churches gradually reappropriated a number of liturgical rites and symbols from the early church, and these changes can be clearly seen in the rituals surrounding the installation of bishops. Miters, copes, and croziers are no longer uncommon, while neckties have largely given way to clerical collars.

In the 1980s, the American Lutheran Church, the Lutheran Church in America, and a breakaway group from the Missouri Synod called the Association of Evangelical Lutheran Churches formed a new unified denomination called the Evangelical Lutheran Church in America (ELCA). It is the largest Lutheran body ever to exist in North America, with nearly 5.5 million members. Like the three bodies that formed it, the ELCA calls its presiding officers bishops. The presiding bishop, with churchwide responsibility, has an office in Chicago.

In the ELCA there are sixty-five synodical bishops, each exercising responsibility in regional areas. As the chief executive officers of the synods they serve, bishops are elected to a six-year term of service, with no limit on reelection, and have a staff of three or four assistants. The bishops meet monthly with an elected body of clergy and laity called the council, chair annual legislative meetings called synod assemblies, and appoint the chairs of all committees, commissions, task forces, and divisions. When there is synod-wide worship, they preside. In terms of their care of clergy, the bishops carry out discipline when clergy go astray, approve all ordinations and new calls to congregations, and personally preside at most ordinations. The bishops use deans—parish pastors elected by conferences (groupings of between eight and twelve local congregations)—to communicate with local clergy. At a national level, the bishops meet together a few times a year as the Conference of Bishops to reflect on issues facing the church and to make recommendations. This body has no legislative authority, nor do the bishops meet as a separate group at the Churchwide Assembly, which is chaired by the national presiding bishop. Bishops are also the chief ecumenical officers of their synods.

Obviously, the bishop has a great deal of responsibility, and not a little authority. However, all policies are set by the legislative assemblies and their implementation is overseen by the council. In the short life of the ELCA, there has not been occasion to deal with a bishop who willfully departed from any major policy. Were it to occur, the national Church Council would have authority to deal with the matter, through the office of the presiding bishop.

An Office in Flux

A preliminary report on Anglican-Lutheran relations put the challenge before the two churches well:

> The functional reality of *episcope* is in flux in both our communions. If we are faithful, we will *together* discover the forms demanded by the church's new opportunities, so that the church may have an *episcope* which will be an *episcope* of the apostolic Gospel. (Lutheran–Episcopal Dialogue I, p. 22)

What does the episcopate need to be to serve a twenty-first-century society? How can our bishops support the church's mission and unity? These are questions best answered by Christians from different traditions exploring them together. Perhaps as Lutherans and Episcopalians embrace a relationship of full communion and a common mission new approaches to episcopacy will be discovered that will be of value to all Christians in the decades to come.

For Reflection

What has been your experience of the ministry of bishops?

What kind of bishops would seem to you to be most useful to the church? Should their administrative role, sacramental role, pastoral role, or their role as symbols of unity be given primary importance? Why?

CHAPTER SIX

THE PRIESTHOOD OF ALL BELIEVERS

Lay and Ordained Ministry in the Church

When we talk about ministry in the church today, we struggle with the same language problem Martin Luther was trying to solve in the Reformation. Luther objected to the way the word "priest" had been confined to ordained people who presided at public worship. No, Luther insisted, all baptized people are priests; the ordained clergy are simply expressing the priesthood of all believers. Today, little has changed. People still use the word "priest" along with the word "minister" as titles for the ordained alone, when in truth we are *all* ministers of the gospel by virtue of our baptism. Luther and the reformers sought to restore the priesthood of all believers emphasized in scripture to the church of their day. And we have also come to realize that all baptized Christians have a priesthood and a ministry. When we talk about ministry, we are talking about the calling of every Christian to serve the world and one another in faithfulness to their Lord.

This calling to ministry is directly related to our baptism, in which we are called to enter a life of Christian learning, witness, and service. Baptism initiates this new life, marked by grace and discipleship. By binding us to Christ's death and resurrection, it frees us to live unafraid of the trials of the world and in joyful service to all God's creation. Cleansed from our sin, we can live without the burden of lingering guilt and shame. The eucharist, likewise, assures us of forgiveness, binds us to our fellow communicants, and points us toward the fulfilled feast of the kingdom of God. The preached Word announces the certainty of the promise of God to redeem and renew us and all creation. It complements the sacramental actions so that we can see, hear, taste, touch, and understand God's grace-filled purpose for our lives. To stress the centrality of baptism, Episcopalians and Lutherans alike now normally baptize at principle services and frequently refer to the significance of baptism in their liturgies.

Despite this convergence of thinking and practice in our two communities, we still often speak of someone "going into the ministry," as if ministry begins with ordination. But ministry includs every baptized person. We learn what ministry is from the life and ministry of Jesus, who is both High Priest and Lord. In his care for all people, regardless of their social status or health or religious practice, Jesus also defined the role of servant in the life of the church and the world. We respond to Christ's ministry by attending to the Word of God and responding to it in faith. This is both the duty and the privilege that accompanies baptism. We are a people who have been ministered to; therefore we become a people who can offer ministry to others.

Lutherans and Episcopalians have similar views on the nature of ministry, though Lutherans tend to stress the "priesthood of all believers" while Episcopalians speak of the "ministry of the baptized." Both agree that all ministry in the church flows from the ministry of Jesus, and is rooted in our identity as people baptized in his name and blessed with his Spirit. At the same time, both the Lutheran and Episcopal churches recognize the importance of calling some members to ordained ministry. By providing formal training for specific ministries of leadership they can assure that the sacramental and liturgical needs of their members are met and that conflict is avoided about what is to be done and who is to do it. Both traditions speak of those ordained as being "empowered" for specific ministries and given gifts of the Spirit for that purpose.

Lay Ministry
The labors of the laity within the setting of the church such as Sunday school teachers, choir members, lay eucharistic ministers, or building committee members are of course good examples of lay ministry. And yet while much of the ministry of the church seems to be service to itself (weekly worship and Christian education for members, for example), such activities are intended to build up the whole people of God for Christian service *in the world*. Ministry is first and fore-

most a form of service to the whole creation. In one of his resurrection appearances to his followers Christ commissioned a body of disciples to continue serving in his name. To this end, he poured out the Holy Spirit upon the faithful to empower them to be his witnesses in the world. Both Lutherans and Episcopalians are explicit in their understanding that the church exists to serve the world. We seek to offer to all people the spiritual gifts that come from Christ, as well as to tend to the physical needs of our neighbors. The four orders of ministers in the church—lay people, bishops, priests/pastors, and deacons—exist to enable the body of Christ to meet those challenges.

Lay ministry begins with the countless ways in which baptized people work and witness in their communities. Living out one's vocation as a Christian at work, in the neighborhood, and in the family is the calling of each lay person in the church. If you have ever had a car break down in a distant city, you know that the calling to be an honest, competent, and courteous mechanic is truly a holy vocation! If you have ever had a prayer with a nurse in a hospital hallway while someone you love was being cared for, then you have experienced the power of laity to be ambassadors of Christ. If a Christian has ever stood by you when others have written you off, you have seen the ministry of the baptized at work. Those who have learned the meaning of compassion, honesty, integrity, and courage as expressions of their baptismal call to serve Christ in other people are able to be effective ministers in the world.

If all the baptized are ministers, in what sense are they "priests"? How do they exercise the "priesthood of all believers"? In ancient religious practice, a priest was someone who could stand between God and the people. The priest would conduct or assist in rituals, offer and consume holy food, speak God's words to the people, and lift the people's petitions to God. They would make sacrifices on behalf of the guilty and offerings on behalf of the grateful. Today, the laity of the church do all these things. They join in the Holy Eucharist as full and equal participants in the divine mystery being offered, and their liturgical roles complement and complete those of the ordained. They speak God's words when they offer words of forgiveness or admonition to their neighbors, or tell the story of Jesus to a child. Their prayers for each other, prayed with the boldness of those who are confident of God's promise to listen, are a kind of offering for those who are burdened with guilt or shame. The laity share their time, their money, and their energy as offerings of gratitude for God's blessings. These marks of priesthood are the signs of lay ministry; they are the church's identifying marks. We are, as Peter said, "a royal priesthood, a holy nation, God's own people," in order that we may proclaim God's mighty acts (1 Peter 2:9).

Lutherans, for historic reasons, have associated the word "priest" with the role of laity, the whole people of God, while Episcopalians have tended to see the priesthood of the whole body expressed in the individual ordained as a priest. Neither church, however, would deny the priesthood of all believers or the importance of calling and ordaining some individuals to express that priestly ministry on behalf of the whole body, particularly in the celebration of the sacraments. It is important to remember, however, that the laity can also play a sacramental role under certain circumstances. In an emergency, for example, any baptized person can baptize another. In marriage also, it is the bride and groom who marry each other by the exchange of vows. The ordained minister prays for them and asks God's blessing on them, but it is they as members of the priestly body who actually "perform" the marriage. The *Lutheran Book of Worship* makes this clear in saying:

> _____ and _____, by their promises before God and in the presence of this congregation, have bound themselves to one another as husband and wife.

Whether lay people may preside at the eucharist is a matter of some controversy in both churches. It has been allowed under certain circumstances in the Lutheran Church but not recommended. Recently, efforts have been made to allow lay people to preside at the eucharist in one part of the Anglican Communion, but these efforts have caused great controversy and so far have been rejected. Nevertheless, the role of lay people in the liturgy has steadily expanded in both churches. Lay assistance in the ministration of communion has become a common experience, and lay people often carry communion to those who are sick and shut-in. All this is simply a working out of the Reformation insight that the eucharist is a corporate action, not an action to be performed by the priest alone. Unless two or three have signified their intention to receive communion, the first *Book of Common Prayer* directs, the eucharist cannot be celebrated. Lay and ordained must act *together* to celebrate their corporate life in Christ.

The Ministry of Priests and Pastors

Having affirmed the importance of the priesthood of all believers and the ministry of the laity that flows from it, it remains true that the ordained also have a vital role to play in the life of the church. In general, ordained ministries are formal, official, specially trained, and usually compensated by the church or a church-run agency. Ordained people are baptized members of Christ's Body, the church, who have been "set apart" for their particular ministries with formal ceremonies and a laying on of hands by other ordained clergy. Neither the Lutheran nor the Episcopal Church has taken an unambiguous stand on the sacramental character of ordination since neither has clearly affirmed more than the two sacraments of baptism and eucharist. In ordination, both churches call on God to confer gifts for ministry on those being ordained, and neither church would ordain someone again if the individual left active ministry for a time. Like baptism, then, it would seem that ordination is an unrepeatable beginning of a specific vocation in the church.

With the establishment of a formal relationship between the Lutheran and Episcopal churches, all ordinations will be at the hands of bishops, though priests and pastors will continue to share in the ordination of new priests or pastors. Most of those who are ordained will serve as local parish clergy (Episcopal priests and Lutheran pastors). Some will be called to serve as bishops, and some clergy will serve in non-parish settings such as hospitals, schools and colleges, prisons, and military chaplaincies.

Medieval parish clergy had served primarily in a sacramental role—baptizing children, blessing marriages, performing last rites, burying the dead, and, above all, standing daily at the altar to say mass. Preaching and teaching were often neglected by priests who were sometimes poorly educated themselves. The reformers insisted that parish clergy were to be instructed in the Bible and able to teach others, with pastoral care and evangelism as priorities. In *The*

Book of Common Prayer ordination service for priests, they were told that they were to be

> Messengers, Watchmen, and Stewards of the Lord; to teach, and to premonish, to feed and provide for the Lord's family; to seek for Christ's sheep that are dispersed abroad...that they may be saved through Christ for ever.

Clergy were to be ordained only with the approval of the congregation and to be examples to their congregations. Their sacramental role is barely mentioned; the reformers believed there was a balance to be corrected.

In the American church today, clergy of all denominations find themselves called to fill roles that neither the early church nor the reformers ever imagined. Now they are also expected to be organizers, community leaders, and fundraisers. Time for prayer and Bible study are easily squeezed out of the schedule unless clergy are disciplined and vigilant. Both Lutherans and Episcopalians, however, have a strong tradition of educated clergy committed to a balanced pastoral ministry of word and sacrament. Together, clergy of the two traditions may be able to adapt this pattern even more effectively to the needs of contemporary American society while offering new models for ordained ministry to the church.

Local parish clergy generally have responsibility for one congregation. In smaller settings, two or three congregations may be served by the same pastor or priest, but the local clergy's duties do not extend to the entire diocese or synod. They preach, teach, baptize, marry, bury, counsel, and more or less provide leadership for the life of a particular congregation in a given town or city. Lutheran clergy confirm, while Episcopalians delegate that responsibility to the bishop, but otherwise expectations of clergy are very similar in the two traditions. Parish clergy see to it that the members of a congregation routinely receive pastoral care and guidance. This can be in the setting of worship, visitation, Bible study, or other means. This ministry is intended to build up the body of Christ for its work in society. Outreach to nonmembers is actually the responsibility of all the members, but frequently falls to the local clergy as well.

Although we have spoken of bishops in a separate chapter, a word needs to be said here about their responsibility of oversight for the clergy in their diocese or synod. For example, in the northeastern United States, the Evangelical Lutheran Church in America has one bishop located in Worcester, Massachusetts, who has oversight duties in all six states of New England. This includes nearly two hundred congregations, all the clergy within the area, and non-parochial ministries, such as campus chaplaincies and church-affiliated nursing homes. The Episcopal Church has seven dioceses in the same six states, each with its own diocesan bishop and various assisting bishops. Each diocese, likewise, has between forty and two hundred congregations and church-run institutions, and a large number of clergy. The responsibility of the bishop in both traditions includes assisting clergy and congregations in times of transition, installation of new clergy, and intervention in congregational disputes. As chief pastors, bishops have particular responsibility to minister to clergy in times of difficulty. Often they may involve others in providing such pastoral care.

It may be useful to notice that the word "hierarchy" is often misused to express a general distrust of clerical authority. This may not seem like an important point, but words can create false impressions. In a democratic society, no one wants "hierarchy." The word "hierarchy" means, literally, "rule by priests," and neither church has that or wants it. Clergy do play an important part in the government of both churches but cannot make important decisions without the consent of the laity. Clergy are called to "ministry," and this does not necessarily involve any administrative or governmental function. Clergy and laity of both churches can, however, assume power beyond what the canons expect in a number of different ways. Sometimes lay people are happy to let clergy run things their way, and sometimes lay people acquire great authority by force of personality or the unwillingness of others to oppose them. The simple existence of such orders as bishop, priest, pastor, or deacon, however, does not in itself constitute an oppressive hierarchical governing of the church by the clergy.

A secular parallel may be the word "bureaucracy," which is also used to express a general distrust of authority. Some bureaucracies may work effectively while others are inefficient and pose a barrier to participation by people in their own government. Likewise, the word "hierarchy" may be used to express a general fear of power being taken from the laity. To the extent that our churches are true to their intentions, they will not put power in the hands of the clergy, but rather will enhance the ministry of the laity and the dignity of the lay office.

Deacons, Deaconesses, and Associates in Ministry
The formal ministry that is in the most exciting period of transition is the diaconate. Both the Episcopal Church and the Evangelical Lutheran Church in America have lately begun to rediscover the role of deacons, as both traditions have been enriched by new

visions of servant ministries. Whether deacons should be ordained remains a significant difference between the churches and another area in which both churches might hope to gain new insights by working together to define servant ministries for the future. The references to deacons in the New Testament are somewhat unclear and the roles they have filled in history have varied widely, though deacons have always been those who expressed in particular the servant ministry of the church.

In the Episcopal Church deacons were historically people in transition to the priesthood. All those ordained to priesthood were ordained first to serve as deacons; the diaconate was even referred to in earlier prayer books as an "inferior ministry." In more recent times, the diaconate has become a significant ministry in its own right, and deacons in the North American Association for the Diaconate have recommended that those called to become priests be ordained directly to the priesthood—as is done in the Lutheran Church of Sweden—so that diaconal ministry would be understood by the church as a specific vocation. While there is wide variation among dioceses, deacons are becoming more numerous in the Episcopal Church and are an important part of the church's ministry. Deacons are trained in theology and servant ministry, and may be assigned to a parish by the bishop to assist in some ministry of service in or near that parish. Because of their involvement in the hopes and needs of the world, it is often the deacon's role on Sunday morning to lead the prayers of intercession.

Prior to the 1970s, when women began to be ordained as deacons and priests, the Episcopal Church set aside (rather than ordained) deaconesses who served as teachers, social workers, and parish visitors. The Lutheran Church likewise has a long history of deaconesses, who have their own community house and discipline. They have mostly functioned as social servants: teachers, nurses, Christian educators, and the like. They remain a small but important part of American Lutheran culture.

Deacons are ordained in some Lutheran churches, such as the Church of Sweden, but although a Lutheran study of ministry published in 1993 advocated the ordination of deacons, after lengthy debate the ELCA chose not to implement that recommendation. Lately, however, other groups of "rostered leaders" have come into being in the Lutheran Church. Diaconal ministers are men and women who are not ordained, nor do they have a specifically disciplined community, as deaconesses do. They may play a number of roles in the life and ministry of the congregation and community, or they may be seen primarily as liturgical assistants. They have some seminary training, and may or may not receive compensation. Associates in Ministry (AIMs) are lay people who, like diaconal ministers, have some seminary training. They work for the church in a wide variety of congregational ministries, such as Christian education, music, and parish nurse programs, and are usually compensated for their services. Some may also work as camp directors or administrators of other church-owned facilities. Because Lutherans link ordination with the sacraments of baptism and communion, only people who preside over these rituals (parish pastors and bishops) are considered ordained.

In the Lutheran Church deacons, deaconesses, and AIMs are commissioned, not ordained. In some areas, diaconal ministry is growing. The Upstate New York Synod, for example, has carefully worked out a program to train and select individuals to serve as deacons, and some parishes have as many as eight serving in that capacity. They assist in worship, visit those in hospitals or special need, make home visits, teach adult and confirmation classes, and serve in social ministries of various kinds. Deacons, AIMs, and deaconesses, like priests and pastors, usually have defined responsibilities not extending beyond their local area or their specific institution.

Speaking in the broadest terms, the Episcopal and Lutheran churches agree that ordained ministry exists to equip the baptized laity for their ministries in the world. This is accomplished by proclaiming the Word of God, that is, the saving biblical word of God to the world, especially in and through the person of Jesus of Nazareth. This proclamation includes both preaching and sacramental actions of the church. Therefore, it is the responsibility of the ordained to see that the spoken and sacramental word of God's grace is regularly available to the baptized people of God. It is the responsibility of the laity to receive these gifts in such a way that they can embody God's grace in their daily lives, especially in relation to the other people who cross their paths.

The Church's Ministry
Our attempt in this chapter to set forth the wide range of ministries in the Episcopal and Lutheran churches reflects the variety of expectations of ordained and lay leaders present in the church today, as well as an evolving view of the role of the baptized. But ministry in Christian tradition is also largely shaped by each person's spiritual gifts. *Charismata* is a New Testament word referring to the special skills and talents of Christian people. Some, as Paul tells us in several places (1 Corinthians and Ephesians), are called to be apostles, prophets, evangelists, pastors, teachers, healers, leaders, and assistants. In other words, Christian

ministry is not simply a mechanical repetition of rituals, nor is it the kind of service that can be dictated by
the whim of a supervisor or board. Ministry occurs
when a Christian brings his or her God-given gifts to
bear upon the specific environment in which that person is living. The person and gifts of the minister,
whether ordained or lay, will profoundly affect the
shape of the ministry that is performed. Some will
have a gift for preaching, while others will have a tal-
ent for counseling or administration or youth work.
Ideally, laity will work togther with clergy to see that
all the gifts of the community are raised up in the service of Christ. Ministry can never adequately be carried
out by one individual. God's gifts are various and no
one individual has them all. The ministries of laity
and clergy are complementary, supplementing and
enhancing each other.

We need to affirm an integrity in ministry that
brings together the ancient faith and traditions of the
church, the unique gifts of the minister, and the particular needs of the world in which the ministry is
being offered. Lutherans and Episcopalians together
may be able to discern and implement more adequately the ministries needed in the world we live in
today than either could do separately.

For Reflection
*What is your understanding of your ministry or role (voca-
tion) in your congregation?*

*Do you feel you are sufficiently challenged, equipped, and
supported to fulfill your role in ministry or leadership?*

CHAPTER SEVEN

OUR COMMON LIFE

Lutheran and Episcopal Congregations

What goes on inside the typical Episcopal or Lutheran church? How do Episcopalians and Lutherans live out their life in Christ? In what ways do they express their baptismal commitment to "continue in the apostles' teaching and fellowship, in the breaking of bread, and in the prayers" (BCP 304). How do they proclaim the gospel in their lives, and seek to serve Christ in all people? What are the customs and traditions that mark our worship and life together? What sense of mission do Episcopalians and Lutherans have? In other words, how do Lutherans and Episcopalians live the gospel today? In this chapter we will describe some of the many different and varied responses to these questions concerning our life in Christian community.

Mission

If you go to your computer and check out the web sites more and more churches are constructing, you will find that most of them have a "mission statement" posted to give inquirers a quick summary of how the congregation sees itself. In an unscientific survey we conducted of some two dozen web sites of churches in each denomination we found a general emphasis on the friendly and welcoming nature most congregations believe themselves to have. Beyond that, there were some differences that may be significant. The shortest and simplest statement from a Lutheran church said: "The friendliest little church in town. Saved by Grace through faith alone." But none of the other Lutheran parish web sites we visited reflected that basic Lutheran theology. A "caring community" and an "extended family" "proclaiming the gospel" were typical phrases. Episcopal churches, similarly, make little reference to the trademark *Book of Common Prayer,* but see themselves also as friendly and family-centered. Episcopal churches, however, are much more likely to use words like "accepting," "inclusive," and "diverse." Some churches noted that they were "multicultural," "gay-friendly," and "welcoming all colors, cultures, and sexual orientations."

Do these somewhat different emphases reflect the different histories of the two churches? The Episcopal Church comes from a background of establishment and may feel itself to be, like the Church of England, a church for everyone in the community. Lutherans, on the other hand, have a European background of separatism and conflict; they arrived in America as cohesive ethnic groups, bound together by language and culture—and separated from other Americans by the very distinctions that united them. Both churches, of course, now see themselves as part of the rapidly changing and diverse American cultural scene and attempt to serve that society in all its various needs. The creation of hospitals, schools, and a wide variety of other social service agencies reflects this concern.

While the influence of the past is still felt, of course, and shapes individual congregations to varying degrees, members of both churches today find themselves grappling with, and torn by, the social issues now being debated in the larger society: wealth and poverty, racism, sexual orientation. Congregations face each of these issues with lesser or greater urgency, depending on whether they are located in urban or rural areas and on the composition of the particular community they serve. Though at times these issues of social justice can be divisive, most Episcopalian and Lutheran communities remain united in their desire to address the spiritual needs of their members created by marital conflict, child-rearing, sickness, and bereavement. Most clergy of both churches see themselves as pastors first, and most congregations see their primary mission as offering support to their members in the joys and sorrows of daily living.

Spiritual Growth

The life of almost all Episcopal churches and Lutheran churches is centered on the worship offered on Sunday mornings. This service will occasionally be Morning Prayer in the Episcopal Church or the first part of the eucharist in a Lutheran Church, but increasingly the Holy Eucharist is the chief act of worship in both. Christian education for both adults and children is also a common part of the Sunday schedule in both churches, with more or less elaborate programs depending on the size of the parish. Our unscientific surf through a number of web sites for both churches revealed a greater likelihood that Lutheran parishes would offer only Bible study on Sunday morning, though ethical issues, contemporary issues, and spirituality were also available in a few places. Episcopal parishes seemed to offer a wider variety of options: groups discussing contemporary issues, contemplative prayer, Christian parenting, and church history, as well as traditional inquirers' classes, were some of the available choices.

Several Episcopal parishes also offered Education for Ministry (EFM), an intensive educational program for members interested in developing their knowledge of the Christian tradition and their ability to serve the church and the world. The program, designed by faculty of the Theological School of the University of the South, requires a commitment of two or three hours a week, nine months a year for four years, and covers such topics as the Bible, church history, and Christian ministry.

Baptisms
Baptism is where parish life, and all Christian life, begins. Our baptism makes us members of Christ and of Christ's body, the church—not Lutherans or Episcopalians or members of a specific denomination. Luther and Cranmer both insisted on the central importance of baptisms. The 1549 prayer book orders that baptisms be performed on Sundays and other holy days when most people can gather, so that the newly baptized can be received into church membership and everyone present will be reminded of their own baptismal commitment. In the same way, Luther's *Large Catechism* emphasizes the importance of a con-

tinuing remembrance of baptism and "what it means truly to plunge into baptism and daily to come forth again."

For all Luther's and Cranmer's good intentions, however, baptism was quickly relegated once again to a corner of Christian experience in both churches. Baptisms seldom occurred at public services, but instead took place in private ceremonies and even in homes instead of in church buildings. It was something that was "done" for every child, but with little preparation or understanding of its meaning. In recent years, both churches have begun again to reclaim baptism as the foundation of the Christian life and to celebrate it at specific times of the year at the main service on Sunday morning or at the Easter Vigil. Both churches also have begun to recreate the catechumenate, which in the early days of the church provided preparation and training for adult converts. Now once again, adult candidates for baptism are received as catechumens, often at the beginning of Lent during the Sunday service, carefully instructed in the faith, and baptized at the Easter Vigil.

Godparents or sponsors (both churches use both terms) should not be overlooked in this discussion. Their role has changed in different periods of church life: sometimes it was a serious responsibility that might well include serving as foster parents or as mentors, while at other times it was little more than a way of honoring friends and relations. Now, once again, the role of godparent is beginning to be taken seriously as an important ministry and a symbol of the fact that the one being baptized is being welcomed into a church family in which the members care for one another.

Confirmation

Confirmation has historically been an important part of church life for both Lutherans and Episcopalians, though for different reasons. Pre-Reformation customs surrounding confirmation varied from place to place with no agreement as to what was essential, though it was usually administered by anointing with oil by the bishop and was often required before admission to communion. Luther saw no value in confirmation but he had no objection to a pastor laying hands on children who had learned the catechism. Cranmer's *Book of Common Prayer* likewise connected confirmation with the catechism, and it became the Anglican practice to require children to learn the catechism and to be confirmed before they could be admitted to communion.

By the twentieth century, confirmation had become a rite of admission to adult membership in the Episcopal Church for children and adults alike, and none were to be admitted to communion until they had been confirmed by the bishop or were "ready and desirous to be confirmed" (a concession of special value in colonial days and on the frontier). Episcopalians were generally taught that confirmation was a "completion" of baptism having to do with the gift of the Holy Spirit. Lutherans, meanwhile, had developed a similar custom of confirmation to mark the completion of instruction in the catechism, but it was administered by the pastor through the laying on of hands. Instruction in the catechism is usually more thorough in the Lutheran than in the Episcopal Church and ordinarily requires two to three years of weekly instruction. Today the ELCA confirmation service is called the Affirmation of Baptism.

By the end of the twentieth century, most scholars in both the Lutheran and Episcopal churches agreed that baptism by itself is sufficient for full church membership and that confirmation has no sacramental significance. Baptized children now are more frequently admitted to communion regardless of their age, and confirmation, where it continues, is treated more as a sign of renewal in faith that might be appropriate for teenagers who wish to reaffirm the baptismal promises made for them as infants or for adults who are returning to the church after a time away. In the Episcopal Church, adults who have not been confirmed are usually asked to participate in an inquirers' class or a similar program, sometimes consisting of only a few meetings with the priest but usually involving a series of six to twelve classes extending over several months. Individuals who have been confirmed in the Roman Catholic Church, by a Lutheran bishop in the historic succession, or anointed in one of the Eastern Orthodox Churches would normally take part in the same program and be received (not confirmed again) by the Episcopal bishop either at a parish visitation or at the diocesan cathedral.

Lutherans today also use a brief series of instructional sessions with the pastor or more formal inquirers' classes. Those coming from other traditions, especially those significantly different, are instructed in Luther's *Small Catechism*, the Augsburg Confession, or some other expression of Lutheran doctrine before being asked if they desire to affiliate themselves with the particular congregation. Adults who have already been confirmed in any Christian tradition are formally welcomed by the pastor using a slight variation of the Affirmation of Baptism service.

Weddings and Funerals
Wedding and funeral customs are probably shaped as much by the society around the churches as by the

church itself. Sometimes even theology can be bent to accommodate culture. Roman Catholics, for example, were for many years not permitted to be cremated, but in Japan, where limited burial space prohibited anything but cremation, an exception was made. Or, in a different vein, if certain music is used for an English royal wedding or a Hollywood wedding, thousands of young couples will want to have the same music whatever theologians or church musicians may think of it. The recent fad for a "unity candle" began in the Roman Catholic Church, but clergy of every church are now asked and even expected to provide one without regard for the questionable theology of the symbolism.

Both *The Book of Common Prayer* and the *Lutheran Book of Worship* provide for the celebration of the eucharist at a wedding or funeral, but the custom seems to be more common in the Episcopal Church. The Episcopal Church requires that at least one party to a marriage be baptized, that the couple be instructed by the priest, and that the bishop's permission be given if one or both parties to the marriage have been previously married and divorced. A Lutheran pastor might also require baptism and instruction or set higher standards, such as evidence of committed church membership, as Episcopal clergy also may and often do, but he or she is not required to do so by canon law. In both churches, the orientation and commitment of the individual clergy person will make a significant difference in the response that is made.

In the event of death, neither church makes any stipulation as to who may or may not have services provided. Some clergy are glad to respond to any request, whatever the individual's religious background, while others feel that their primary commitment is to members of the congregation and prefer not to spend time on those without any church connection. The prayer books of both churches provide a funeral service that can include the eucharist or not. *The Book of Common Prayer* directs that the coffin be closed before the church service begins and that earth be cast on the coffin at the grave. The *Lutheran Book of Worship* says nothing about a closed coffin (though it is customary), and suggests the casting of earth on the coffin but leaves such practice to the pastor's discretion.

Music

Christians use a wide variety of music in their worship, but visitors to Episcopal and Lutheran churches will find many similarities. The treasuries of majestic German and English choral music and the sweet melodies of British and Scandinavian folk tunes form the basis for a moving collection of hymns. Both churches have freely borrowed from each other for over a hundred years. In addition, newer music from American composers and an influx of hymnody from developing countries is enriching the congregational singing of both traditions. It should be noted that the practice of strong lay hymn singing has been part of both communions since their beginning. Indeed, congregational singing is one of the hallmarks of the Reformation. Lutheran and Anglican worship has only grown in its commitment to vital congregational singing.

The liturgical texts are often chanted, too. This may be slightly more common in Lutheran parishes than Episcopal, but both maintain strong traditions of chanted liturgy. In most Lutheran churches now there are at least two books, the *Lutheran Book of Worship* and a newer, more contemporary resource called *With One Voice*. Between these two, there are six distinct chant settings for the liturgy. While the Lutheran books contain complete service texts including the music, Episcopalians turn to a separate book, *The Hymnal 1982,* for hymns and service music. In many parishes, the better known chants are simply sung from memory. For the visitor, the chants of the two traditions can be difficult to pick up quickly; it may take several visits to a particular parish to learn the setting that is used and join in the congregational responses. Thus it might be worthwhile if two congregations are doing regular exchanges to introduce the music before the joint worship begins. An evening program around a pot-luck meal learning each other's *Kyries, Glorias, Agnus Deis,* and *Sanctuses* could be fun, informative, and provide a smoother series of common worship times.

Both churches also commonly enjoy additional music in the form of choral or solo anthems, or instrumental music with, or instead of, the traditional organ. In all musical choices, both churches will tend toward well-composed, formal, even classical styles, though more contemporary rhythms will be heard in some places. Generally, both Anglican and Lutheran church music focuses on the grand themes of God's great work of salvation. One of the three persons of the Trinity (Father, Son, or Holy Spirit) will usually be the subject.

Scriptural stories or psalms provide the basis for many hymns, canticles, or anthems. Where humans are the subject, our two traditions will often refer to the whole church or the whole world. With a few exceptions, Anglicans and Lutherans shy away from songs that emphasize an individual's special relationship to God. A wide array of this type of religious music came out of the various revivals and pietistic movements over the centuries. While often popular, the emphasis on "me and Jesus" tends to downplay the grander sense of God's covenant with all humanity, and with the whole people of Christ. Instead of focusing on *my* trust in God, most Anglican and Lutheran church music lifts up *God's* trustworthiness in the mighty promises and deeds of the scriptural drama.

Liturgical Traditions and Parish Customs

A cartoon in the *New Yorker* magazine some years ago showed a small boy standing at his father's knee as his father explained, "But, son, we WASPs have no ethnic traditions." In fact, however, if it seems that Lutherans, Episcopalians, and other Christians of northern European background "have no ethnic traditions," it is only because their ethnic traditions now belong to everyone. Santa Claus came to America with the Dutch but can now be found even in non-Christian countries like Japan. The Advent wreath seems to have German origins but is now used by Roman Catholics and Baptists. The Christmas tree as we know it originated in western Germany and was popularized in England by Queen Victoria's German husband, Prince Albert. Today even Jewish families sometimes set up Christmas trees because everyone else does and it has no specifically Christian meaning.

Lutherans and Episcopalians are part of the predominant culture that has shaped American Christianity and American life. Traditions that were once uniquely English, German, or Scandinavian are now part of the general culture. In churches as free as the Lutheran and Episcopal, moreover, it is almost impossible to make assertions about either church that will have no exceptions. They do, however, have some traditions and customs—often with no real theological meaning—that may throw some light on what it means to belong to one church or the other.

Before the Reformation, the colors used to mark the changing seasons varied widely and there were no rules to follow. Most of England, for example, followed the customs of Salisbury Cathedral in using unbleached linen in Lent and bleached linen for Easter, while Rome used purple during Lent. The churches in other countries followed various local customs: some used black for Christmas and feasts of the Virgin Mary and blue for Epiphany and Ascension. Yellow and green were used interchangeably in England. After the Reformation, however, the use of liturgical colors gradually died out in the reformed churches while Rome imposed its own pattern as far as possible. Thus, when English and German Christians looked for ways to enrich their services in the nineteenth and twentieth centuries, they found only one pattern to copy and that was the Roman tradition. For a while, any church using colored vestments in Advent or Lent used purple.

As liturgical scholars in the twentieth century studied matters more deeply, however, they rediscovered a variety of long-forgotten regional customs. Some Anglicans began again to use the old English tradition of blue in Advent instead of purple and off-white materials in Lent. Surprisingly, despite their concern for a common pattern of worship, Episcopalians have never provided either rules or guidance on the subject of liturgical colors and Episcopal churches are free to do as they like. The *Lutheran Book of Worship* does offer guidance, suggesting essentially the same colors as those used by Roman Catholics and most other western churches. Both Episcopalians and Lutherans, however, are free to do as they like in this area, following what has become the common tradition or using alternatives that seem helpful to clergy and congregations.

By the time of the Reformation, a standard pattern of clergy dress in the liturgy had developed in western Europe. Clergy wore vestments that had evolved from the ordinary clothes of citizens in the days of the Roman empire. After the Reformation these vestments slowly disappeared in England and were then reintroduced in the mid-nineteenth century. Lutheran usage varied widely from one country to another. In Sweden the traditional vestments were retained, while in other countries they were generally abandoned. Lutheran settlers in America thus had very different experiences to draw on and kept a variety of customs, ranging from the most elaborate vestments to none at all.

In the course of the twentieth century this variety was greatly reduced and the vestments of Lutheran clergy today are often almost identical to those of Episcopal clergy, though Lutherans are probably less likely to use the traditional medieval vestments than Episcopalians. In recent years the shape and use of traditional vestments has further evolved: the long vestment called an alb, which was once always white and worn under a colored chasuble, has emerged in what is called "wheat" color and become a standard vestment of many Protestant and Roman Catholic clergy alike. A long, narrow stole in the seasonal colors or a rainbow of designs is often worn over the alb. It is no longer easy to tell what church you are in by the vestments worn. Lutherans and Episcopalians are probably more similar and more traditional in this area than clergy of other churches, but wide variety can be found and no generalizations are safe.

Clergy titles are also a matter of custom; no church rules require that clergy be called by one title or another. That Lutheran clergy are generally called "Pastor" seems to reflect Luther's concern to emphasize the pastoral, as opposed to the priestly, role of the clergy. The use of "Father" or "Mother" for Episcopal clergy is relatively modern, as it is in the Roman Catholic Church; in the Middle Ages the titles referred only to members of religious orders. Some Episcopalians have never been comfortable with the titles and have questioned whether a word that implies patriarchal or matriarchal authority really represents the ideal relationship between priests and lay people. The wearing of clerical collars and black shirts for priests and purple shirts for bishops is also a matter of preference. No rules in either church require any particular way of dressing for clergy.

Membership
Both the Lutheran and Episcopal churches are clear that baptism makes one a member of the church. In practice, however, not everyone baptized in the church actively lives out that membership, participating regularly in worship and working with other Christians to witness to God's love, serve God's church, and minister to those in need. Churches therefore have needed to maintain membership lists of those who are active members of the Christian community. Episcopalians and Lutherans define that active membership in similar but somewhat different ways.

In both churches, those who are baptized in the church are listed as members of the church until they die or are transferred. Neither church, however, would report everyone who has ever been baptized as an active member. That status, which is important for voting at parish meetings and assessing the real membership of a parish or of the whole church, is reserved by both churches for those who give annual evidence of commitment. Lutherans define active membership as those who are "confirmed, communing and contributing" and define "communing" as including those who have received communion at least once in the last year. "Contributing" involves a financial contribution of record. The equivalent status in the Episcopal Church is that of a "communicant member in good standing": one who has received communion at last three times in the past year and has been "faithful in working, praying, and giving for the spread of the kingdom of God."

Parish Names

There are no rules about what name a congregation chooses for itself but there are traditions that can hint at a parish's denominational pedigree. Both Episcopal and Lutheran congregations often choose the names of the apostles: Saints Peter, John, Paul, and Matthew are especially popular. Only a handful use female names, such as Mary or Mary Magdalene. Sometimes Lutheran parishes will be named for such Scandinavian saints as St. Olaf of Norway, while newer Episcopal churches often take names from their English heritage, such as St. Bede, St. Alban, and St. Dunstan. Both Episcopalians and Lutherans use the titles of Jesus—Christ, Redeemer, Good Shepherd, and Messiah. Both will use names of seasons such as Advent, Nativity, or Epiphany. Resurrection and Ascension are not uncommon. Trinity and Holy Cross are quite common to both denominations, as are Grace and Faith. Occasionally Lutherans use a Latin name such as *Gloria Dei* or names of spiritual gifts, such as Peace or Hope. If one of our congregations has a number in its name, such as First or Second, it is almost certainly a Lutheran congregation. It is also invariably Lutheran if it uses a name derived directly from the German Reformation: Augustana (a version of Augsburg), Concordia, Luther, or Reformation.

Biblical place names, such as Zion, Bethany, and Bethlehem, are often used by Lutherans. If the name has a hyphen, such as St. Mark's-by-the-Sea, it is almost always Episcopal. Also, Episcopalians are more likely to leave out the word "Episcopal" when referring to their congregation. For example, if someone says "I belong to Christ Church," it will most likely mean an Episcopal parish. If the person is a Lutheran, he or she will say "I belong to Christ Lutheran," often omitting the word "church." We can see that one of the pitfalls of future joint missions may well involve naming the new parish: imagine trying to find the congreation of "St. Hedwig's-Reformed-Evangelical-Lutheran-Episcopal-Under-the-Overpass"!

More seriously, what these names reveal is a deep appreciation of the scriptural tradition. The vast majority of names for our congregations reflect traditional themes of biblical faith, or names of later martyrs for that faith. While some of our parishes use the name of the town in which they are placed, most prefer to lift up some reminder of our ancient heritage. Our names tend to reflect the common sense of identity that is founded upon the apostles' witness to God's saving work as reflected in the Bible.

A few words might be said here about the terms "Protestant" and "Catholic." A few generations ago, when Americans were asked to name a religious preference a great majority would have used one of three words: Protestant, Catholic, or Jewish. Jewish encompassed all of the major branches of Judaism, including non-practicing "cultural Jews." Catholic referred to Roman Catholics, and Protestant was the word that took in all other Christians. The word "Protestant" was used both to affirm and to denounce. It affirmed a general acceptance of Reformation principles such as the authoritative role of scripture, a strong role for lay people, a more or less democratic decision-making process, a fair amount of congregational autonomy, and a certain freedom in doctrinal interpretation and in the practice of ceremonies and rituals. It was also used negatively in opposition to anything perceived as "Romish": centralized church authority, the pope, mechanical and uniform ritual, any special status for clergy, an external hierarchy, or any supremacy of tradition over scripture. The word was used to include any non-Roman Catholic Christians, including Southern Baptists, Methodists, Congregationalists, Lutherans, Episcopalians, and Presbyterians, to name just a few.

Many of the changes that have been described in this book have brought about a rethinking of our religious categories, especially the terms protestant and catholic. Episcopalians have long cherished the word "catholic" but today the term is being reclaimed by others as well, as a word that describes those who are eager to maintain the ancient, traditional, apostolic faith. To be catholic is to appreciate, and often to appropriate, the very rich tradition of the whole church. It means to read authors who wrote between A.D. 200 and 1600 and to reflect upon their collective and faithful wisdom. It means to study early liturgies to see how they sought to communicate the faith, and to consider the structure of Christian communities in the early centuries of the church, to see how the Spirit was working through them. In short, it means that our faith today assumes that the whole two thousand years of Christian history contains much of value which we must reclaim and maintain, and which we must transmit if we are to be fully the Body of Christ. To be catholic does not require that we jettison the insights of the Reformation, but it does affirm that the German and English reformations did not intend to jettison the great tradition from which they both emerged.

To the extent that "protestant" refers to resistance to abuses of church power, either in the sixteenth century or in our own time, then the Episcopal and Lutheran churches would qualify for that label. But if protestant has come to mean using the Bible in a way that Luther warned about, as a "paper Pope," or treating each congregation as if it existed apart from every other, or acting as if each person's experience or opinion should be seen as representing the apostolic faith, then neither the Anglican nor Lutheran traditions would qualify. If to be protestant in America today means to substitute entertainment for liturgy, or to rely on personal self-expression above historic creeds, or to demand strict adherence to a narrow set of "fundamentals" apart from the patient discernment of the Spirit's movement through the variegated texture of the church's long life, then Lutherans and Episcopalians will not consider the word protestant as an apt description. In some quarters, mostly among students of church history, the terms "reformed catholic" and "evangelical catholic" are being more commonly used to describe both Anglican and Lutheran strands of Christianity. These terms are at least an attempt to recover the distinctive stance of Christians who deeply value their apostolic heritage but insist on whatever continuing reforms are needed to keep the promise of the gospel of God's grace in the center of the church's life.

Social Ministries
The differences in the social ministries of the two churches would seem to be a result of their distinct historical development. Episcopalians are better represented in the large cities, especially on the east coast,

and began developing hospitals and other social agencies in the middle of the nineteenth century. The largest food program in the world, for example, is operated by the Church of the Holy Apostles in New York City. Food pantries, after-school programs, women's shelters, and other ministries to those in need are common activities now of both churches. Most parishes of both churches, in rural as well as urban communities, are probably involved in some way in such programs today.

At a national level both churches have effective organizations to coordinate ministries both at home and abroad. A well-developed network of Lutheran agencies, Lutheran Social Services, serves the developmentally disabled and works through nursing homes, adoption agencies, and counseling services. The Lutheran World Federation coordinates disaster relief.

The Episcopal Church reaches out in worldwide ministry through Episcopal Relief and Development (formerly known as the Presiding Bishop's Fund for World Relief), which focuses on programs to encourage development rather than simply responding to emergencies. Within the United States, health and welfare agencies are sponsored by both dioceses and parishes. The annual church directory lists hundreds of agencies: hospitals, housing agencies, retirement homes, counseling centers, shelters for runaways and abused spouses, ministries to immigrants and seafarers, crisis ministries, and many more. In recent years the Episcopal Church has developed a network of over five hundred Jubilee Centers, parishes recognized for leadership programs of evangelism, outreach, empowerment, and advocacy.

Many factors affect a given congregation's "personality." Clearly, the clergy who serve the parish bring their own priorities and passions to their ministry. The proximity to other congregations and the sense of similarity or distinctiveness in relation to those parishes will affect church life. In communities where there are several churches of one tradition, each may take on a special character and become known for its music, its preaching, or its social witness. The number of recent new members from other traditions will make some patterns of congregational life easier and others harder. Any contacts the parish has had with its bishop's office, whether positive or negative, will affect many attitudes and practices. All these factors cross denominational lines. What is important is that our parishes need to be willing to relate to each other as they really *are*. Experiences, especially if they are negative, from other places or past times should not be allowed to deter us or determine our future ministry together. What we have been and what we are is not necessarily what God will have us be.

For Reflection
What specific people and events in your church of origin helped shape your Christian faith and understanding of your role in the life of the church when you were young?

What people and events in your present parish shape your ongoing spiritual life?

Does the pattern of your parish's life address most of the central concerns and desires you have as a member of a Christian community?

CHAPTER EIGHT

THE FUTURE CHURCH

Toward Christian Unity

Now let's dream. Through almost five hundred years, the life of the Christian church has been dominated by division. The energies that might have been used to transform our society have been used instead to defend one denominational system against another. While Christian mission has indeed reached to the ends of the earth, schools and hospitals have been built, and the needs of the poor have not been entirely overlooked, imagine what might have been done if the Christians of the world had been able to work together toward common goals. Imagine what we might accomplish in the future, as Lutherans and Episcopalians unite in common mission.

One of the most exciting aspects of the new Lutheran-Episcopal relationship is the way both churches are reexamining everything from a new perspective and asking, "Could we do this better together?" Representatives of both churches involved with issues of corporate responsibility have already met to consider joint actions that would benefit all. A Lutheran jurisdiction that overlaps several Episcopal dioceses may join in a self-insurance program that one of the Episcopal dioceses has used successfully for its buildings. Another Episcopal diocese that includes the same territory as one Lutheran synod has suggested the possibility of a shared cathedral and office building. Still another Episcopal diocese has invited Lutherans to share in its diaconal training program. Long ago someone said that churches should never do separately what they can do together. Perhaps we should now ask whether there is anything that we cannot do better together, with the greater resources and advantages of broader experience our cooperation brings. Together we can be better witnesses to who we are: the Body of Christ, united in ministry and worship.

In this chapter we would like to offer several suggestions for changes that could be made to express and enhance our common mission in the future. These ideas are only a beginning of the exploration we Lutherans and Episcopalians will be engaged in for years to come.

A Common Prayer Book
One obvious place to begin is with prayer books. While Anglicans have long based their unity on a common prayer book, Lutherans in America have recently

found that a common book for worship soon produced unity between separate Lutheran churches. Both churches now have useful books issued within the last generation. Both also have alternative liturgies that are widely used and they have been discussing the possibility of revising their standard books. Is not this, then, the perfect time for the two churches to appoint a committee charged with producing a new prayer book for optional use in both churches? A single book for worship would be an ideal way to signal and solidify the new relationship between the two churches. When members of either church visit the other and find a familiar prayer book in the pew, they will see that the members of this "other" church are not that different. And if we can pray together, we will grow closer and be enabled to act on our common mission in a variety of other ways.

It might even be possible to take this proposal further and invite other churches into the project. Lutherans have a covenant relationship with the churches of the Reformed tradition, for example. Would it be possible to share a prayer book with them as well, and so take one step closer to still another separated part of Christ's body?

Seminaries
Another important area in which the Lutheran and Episcopal churches can begin to act in common mission involves the theological schools or seminaries that prepare men and women for ordained ministry. Seminaries of both churches need to expose their students to the history, theology, and worship of the other. It is said that common mission has to be local to be real, and parish clergy need to be educated about other churches in order to lead parishioners in effective common action. Some seminaries of both

churches have, in fact, already begun to explore ways in which they can cooperate and to put programs in place.

Exchange professorships are one obvious and easy step to take. Students might be encouraged—or even required—to spend a period of time at a seminary of the other denomination. Going further, if the stereotype that Lutherans are better at theology while Episcopalians are better at liturgy is true, would it be useful to have a Lutheran teach Episcopalians theology and an Episcopalian teach liturgy to Lutherans? Conversely, might it not be useful for Lutherans to study theology with an Episcopal scholar to discover another way of doing theology, and might not Episcopalians have their horizons broadened by studying the "evangelical freedom" of Lutheran liturgical customs?

With a few exceptions, most of the seminaries of the two churches are not in competition since they serve different geographical areas. In a time when many seminarians are married and have roots in a community, it may be helpful to some to have the option of attending a seminary nearer home. The Episcopal Church, for example, has two seminaries in New England where there is no Lutheran seminary. Lutheran seminarians in that area might be able to attend an Episcopal seminary for at least part of their education, especially if the Episcopal seminary were to create a Lutheran studies program to supplement their usual course offerings. Episcopalians in such a seminary would benefit also from the opportunity to learn more about their sister communion.

Bishops
While the seminaries of the two churches can train future leaders to work together, so the existing leader-

ship can explore ways to unite the work of the churches now. The bishops of both churches meet as a body
at least annually to consult about issues facing their
church. The opportunities for common mission need
to be explored in such meetings, and joint meetings of
the two conferences of bishops are an essential ingre-
dient in that exploration. As the bishops meet together, pray together, and study common issues together
new possibilities will emerge and plans for action can
be put in place.

For bishops, the competing demands of the pastoral and the administrative aspects of their calling are
a source of constant tension. One area that might be
explored, then, is the possibility that Lutheran and
Episcopal bishops could support each other by filling
roles their colleagues cannot. An example of this is the
need priests and pastors have for a chief pastor and
the conflict implicit in seeking pastoral care from the
same bishop who has such influence over their
careers. But if an Episcopal priest facing marital or
pastoral problems feels uncomfortable in talking to
his or her own bishop, perhaps the Lutheran bishop
could be the pastor they need; the Episcopal bishop
could serve the same role for a Lutheran pastor.

Simply in geographical terms there may also be
opportunity for mutual support and cooperative ministry among bishops. In New England the Episcopal
Church has seven dioceses with ten bishops, while the
Lutheran Church has one synod and one bishop. In
Minnesota, on the other hand, there are six Lutheran
synods and one Episcopal diocese. These are large
areas for a single bishop to cover. In a pastoral emergency it might be much easier for a bishop of the
other church to be available than one's own.

Evangelism

Evangelism has many faces but there is no reason why Episcopalians and Lutherans should present different faces in their efforts to spread the gospel. Both churches have had successful radio and television programs, for example, but the costs of such ventures are high and cooperation might make the programs more effective. Planning together for the building of new churches or maintaining old ones ought also to be an area of productive cooperation. In some places buildings are already being shared; in still others, a Lutheran and an Episcopal church contribute toward the ministry of one priest or pastor. In small dying towns or in decaying inner cities, the resources of two churches combined ought to enable more effective ministry than the two churches can provide separately, perhaps even helping to turn such neighborhoods around. In areas of new growth, the two churches might also cooperate to meet expanding needs. It may be that Lutherans and Episcopalians can begin to grow together at the parish level, even while remaining separate churches at the regional and national level.

Parish Life

Imagine the church in perhaps fifty years from now—or possibly only five. Christians enter the church building with its signboard speaking of both Lutherans and Episcopalians. As they settle into their pews they find their place in the worship book—one that has been jointly published by the Evangelical Lutheran Church in America and the Episcopal Church. The prayer book contains two or three mutually agreed settings for the Holy Eucharist, a set of occasional services, and a common collection of great hymns. The clergy who lead the service may be either

Episcopal or Lutheran or both, but their seminary educations have been built around a strong, common curriculum. Indeed, some seminaries have actually merged to form a single school that reflects both traditions. The parish Sunday school has both Episcopal and Lutheran students, and uses jointly published materials. The youth group meeting that afternoon also includes members of both congregations, as does the group of soup kitchen volunteers who go together to serve their neighbors. The part of the offering that supports social ministries is not divided, but funds projects operated by a joint commission of both communions.

In this church of the future dioceses and synods have been rearranged so that where Lutherans are concentrated the few Episcopal congregations are overseen by a Lutheran bishop, and where Episcopalians are more numerous Lutheran parishes are overseen by Episcopal bishops. Regional and national conventions regularly use teachers and preachers from the other church as keynote presenters, workshop facilitators, or worship leaders. Local parish councils and vestries have annual retreats together. Stewardship and evangelism training is done jointly. Shared worship space and services are the norm.

In a church as united as the one we have described the question of why we would want to remain two separate denominations might well arise. It is certainly not unthinkable that mergers between congregations will combine communities that are now distinct. But merging into a single body is not the only model for living out this new relationship between the Lutheran and Episcopal churches. With all that we share, we still have certain cultural differences between us that we may wish to retain. If so, one way to imagine the future is to think of the present structure of religious orders within Roman Catholicism. Franciscans and Jesuits are very different in their organization, methodology, and missionary objectives, but they are in full eucharistic fellowship and mission. They are organized as distinct bodies, each with its own pattern of oversight, theological and liturgical emphases, training, and ministry. They may even compete for new members. Yet they are members of one church. So in the future Lutheran and Episcopal Christians might see themselves as something like two orders within the larger church. They would not be in competition; indeed, they would cooperate in every way that they could. But they would bring the richness of their histories and their unique perspectives into the common life of the church. The Anglican emphasis on liturgy, creation, and incarnation needs to be continually embraced within the whole church catholic, as does the Lutheran focus on the gospel and the freedom that is enjoyed by sinners who have been justified by grace and who live that new life through faith. As the two groups grow together, each may continue to be true to its own history and emphases while intentionally incorporating the best features of the other into its life.

Even now there are some very practical steps we can take to make this vision a reality. Look at something as basic as the service schedule. The increasing diversity of our communities makes it difficult for every member to gather once or twice on Sunday, as they did a century ago. Sunday mornings in our society have become so crowded with work, school, and family activities that many larger congregations are discovering the advantages of adding a Saturday evening service, often with a shared meal and a more leisurely opportunity for Christian education afterward. A midweek service can serve that purpose, too, but some congregations might not be able to offer such choices without further dividing an already small community. Jointly planned and conducted services, on the other hand, could create more opportunities for worship and increased understanding between the churches. A Saturday evening service, for example, might be held at the church with the liturgies alternating between those of the two churches. Midweek services might be offered at an early hour by one church and at noon or early evening by the other.

Church staffs might be strengthened also by the sharing of resources. Where churches are growing slowly and budgets are still tight, the calling of a third clergy person to augment the ministry in two neighboring congregations could now be considered as a project jointly planned and supported. Combining worship on so-called "low Sundays" or during clergy vacations may also be an effective way to build our relationship. Adult scripture study, men's and women's groups, and other programs that might be poorly attended if sponsored by one church would have a fuller attendance when offered jointly. The chance to share insights about the faith with those of a different tradition would be an additional bonus.

Clergy
Our clergy could also work together as pastoral teams in a particular area. In a congregation whose priest or pastor is male, for example, would it not make sense to ask the female priest or pastor of a neighboring parish to be available for pastoral care for those parishioners who would be better served by a woman—and vice versa? In the same way, the ethnic and cultural distinctions of the clergy in one parish could enrich the worship and pastoral ministry of a neighboring congregation. Or imagine a situation in

which one clergy person is very good at bereavement counseling and another is specially trained in marriage and premarital work. Would it not make sense to refer most of the bereavement counseling to one and most of the marriage counseling to the other? Could our clergy not immediately begin to use each other as mentors, confessors, or for peer support in times of congregational change or stress?

In recent years, lawsuits and lurid stories of clergy misconduct have become common. Clearly clergy in all church bodies need assistance, both to prevent and also to correct improper behavior. Presently when a cleric is accused of some malfeasance, an investigation of the charges is made by someone from the bishop's office in the diocese or synod in which ministry is being performed. This raises an immediate conflict because the bishop, who is supposed to be the pastor to the local pastor, is also the one who will administer the discipline. The tension and distress can be quite powerful, but imagine how the situation might be defused if a Lutheran investigated and recommended a discipline for Episcopal clergy who misbehaved, and vice versa. A well-trained colleague from another tradition can bring a more objective perspective, especially if the one being investigated has been at odds with the bishop or has been a close friend. We could even create a team of specially trained people from both churches who would automatically receive referrals when someone was accused and work together in a way that both respected the bishop's pastoral role and offered a more impartial approach than an "in-house" system could do.

But it is neither wise nor necessary to wait for problems to arise. Suppose, for example, that every newly ordained clergy person were assigned a mentor from the other communion. Because there would be no chance of this mentor ever becoming bishop in the new clergy person's diocese (or the other way around), the mentor could be trusted with deep struggles of faith and personal issues of a sensitive nature. This kind of collegial support could well prevent serious misconduct from occurring.

Parish Leadership

It is not only clergy who need support and ongoing training. Local vestries and councils would also benefit from attending occasional retreats or planning meetings with leaders from a congregation of the other tradition. Sunday school teachers and stewardship committees from Lutheran and Episcopal congregations could receive training together, and larger, blended youth groups could sponsor more creative recreational and service projects, especially in small parishes. Worship and music workshops could include leaders of both congregations. Special festivals or worship events that have not been part of a local tradition could be more successfully introduced if offered together. At least part of confirmation studies for young people and adults could be shared, utilizing again the particular skills of the clergy of both churches.

Toward Christian Unity

Episcopalians can make some claim to being pioneers in the ecumenical movement. It was the Episcopal Church that challenged the other churches well over a hundred years ago to consider uniting on the basis of four fundamentals: the Bible, the ancient creeds, the two sacraments Christ instituted, and a threefold ministry in historic succession. Through the second half of the twentieth century, a variety of American churches have been in conversation about unity on this basis, but without lasting results. Proposals have been drawn up to unite the churches involved but have always foundered for one reason or another.

Anglicans may have an optimistic attitude toward ecumenism because it has always seemed to them that the same worship-centered unity that has worked for Anglicanism should also work for others. A generation ago, Episcopalians in New York City could find parishes worshiping in a variety of styles, ranging from the simplest service of Morning Prayer to the most elaborate celebration of the eucharist, yet all the liturgies came from the same prayer book. Why, Episcopalians wondered, was this not a path that others could follow? Unity in worship—actually, a wide variety of ceremonial patterns but all from the same book—allowed room also for great theological diversity. There was freedom to explore and change and grow on the basis of a shared pattern of worship. It was an Episcopalian, Canon Edward West of New York's Cathedral of St. John the Divine, who designed a shield for the Anglican Communion featuring the words "The truth shall make you free."

Evangelical freedom, on the other hand, has also been a watchword for Lutherans. It seemed to them that the best way to unite Christians was to agree on a statement of faith. Without question, that approach has been effective in uniting Lutherans in this country, overcoming a great variety of ethnic differences and diverse liturgical styles. Only recently have Lutherans had sufficient unity among themselves to test that approach on a wider basis, but the results have been impressive. Mutual recognition has been attained with churches of the Reformed tradition, including the Presbyterian Church U.S.A., the United Church of Christ, and the Reformed Church in America, as well as with the Moravian Church and, of course, the

Episcopal Church. Perhaps more impressive still was the signing of a mutually agreed statement with the Roman Catholic Church on the doctrine of justification, the very issue that first set Martin Luther in conflict with the pope.

Thus the Episcopal Church and the Evangelical Lutheran Church in America have both shown a determination to work toward Christian unity and have found in their own fundamental traditions a principle around which that unity might be sought. Both churches also have emphasized freedom as an essential element in the life of the Christian church. The fact that Lutherans have stressed theological unity and liturgical freedom while Episcopalians have stressed liturgical unity and theological freedom might seem to produce a certain creative tension between them. Episcopalians may worry about Lutheran liturgical freedom just as Lutherans worry about Episcopal theological freedom, but mutual recognition and appreciation have been gained nonetheless.

On either side of the Lutheran and Episcopal churches, however, are other churches that find their unity not in liturgy or theology or freedom, but rather in authority. The Roman Catholic tradition looks to the authority of the pope as the basis of unity, while a variety of protestant churches claim the authority of the Bible as the sole basis of unity. Can we learn something from them about discipline and faithfulness? Perhaps so—and we have gifts we believe could be of great value to them as well. As Lutherans and Episcopalians talk together and come to understand each other better, we need to bear in mind the greater challenge that still lies ahead and look for elements that can be useful in working toward still greater Christian unity. The common witness to freedom in unity that these two churches have to offer might, as they make effective common witness, help other Christians also find the gifts God has given us to share.

Called to Common Mission

"What difference will it make," asked Stephen Paul Bouman, ELCA Bishop of the New York Metropolitan Synod, "if Anglicans and Lutherans—who really believe that we eat and drink in the midst of the graveyard for the life of the world—come together?" Will this make it possible for the hopeless, the homeless, the prisoners "to catch a glimpse of God" in the places where they live their lives? "Will we sponsor deacons and others in places no one else will go? If that's not what CCM is about," he declared, "it's not worth the hassle!"

Surely the fact that the agreement between the two churches is named Called to Common Mission is a challenge to both churches to live out the faith they profess in new ways that make a real difference, not only within the churches but also in the communities around them. Will those communities see our parishes embrace more fully the mission of the church to proclaim the gospel and address the needs and concerns of the poor, the homeless, the sick, and those in prison? If not, the effort made to sign an agreement has accomplished little of lasting value.

We have noted in this book that Anglicans have tended to emphasize the incarnation and therefore the celebration of the Christmas mystery, while Lutherans have tended to focus on Christ's saving death and the remembrance of Good Friday. The challenge before us, then, might be described as learning to celebrate Easter and Pentecost together, and to find ways to share the gift of new life and the power of the Spirit with a world that needs those gifts.

For Reflection

If you could change anything in your local church or denomination, what would it be? What would your ideal church look like?

Why would you make those changes? What would it take to make those changes happen?

RESOURCES FOR FURTHER STUDY

A complete education program is available from LeaderResources to assist congregations, dioceses, and synods in using this book to explore the relationship between the two denominations. This resource includes:

- Leader's guide for Sunday or weekday adult education programs of various lengths
- Lesson plans for youth and children, including shared ministry activities
- Events and activities for two or more congregations to share
- Local and international pilgrimages
- Plans for regional clergy or lay gatherings
- A process to explore ways to share programs, clergy, space, or worship
- An introduction to each denomination's key education programs and resources
- A copy of the official text of Called to Common Mission

- Information about each denomination's structure and organization

To obtain more information or to order the education resource call:

LeaderResources
800-941-2218
staff@LeaderResources.org
www.LeaderResources.org
38 Mulberry Street, Leeds, MA 01053

EPISCOPAL

The Anglican Vision, James E. Griffiss (Cowley, 1997), $11.95. An introduction to the Anglican tradition, its origins and development, and its ability to hold together theological continuity and cultural change.

A Brief History of the Episcopal Church, David Holmes (Trinity Press International, 1993), $17.00.

A User's Guide to the Holy Eucharist, Chrisopher L. Webber (Morehouse, 1997), $7.00. A page by page commentary on the prayer book service.

The Book of Common Prayer (Church Publishing, 1979). The pew edition is $14.95 and the 1982 *Hymnal* is $18.95.

Opening the Prayer Book, Jeffrey Lee (Cowley, 1999), $11.95. An historical survey of *The Book of Common Prayer* and why it developed as it did.

The Challenge of Change: The Anglican Communion in the Post-Modern Era, Mark Harris (Church Publishing, 1998), $19.95. A study of issues of authority and identity in the

Anglican Communion as it explores a vision for the future.

Welcome to the Episcopal Church, Christopher L. Webber (Morehouse, 1999), $11.95. An introduction to the history, worship, and teaching of the Episcopal Church.

LUTHERAN

Fortress Introduction to Lutheranism, Eric W. Gritsch (Augsburg Fortress, 1993), $15.00. A look at the history and themes of Lutheranism.

Day by Day We Magnify Thee: Daily Readings for the Entire Year, Martin Luther (Augsburg Fortress, 1982), $22.00. Daily meditations on scripture, giving good insight into Luther's spirituality.

Here I Stand: A Life of Martin Luther, Roland Bainton (Abingdon-Cokesbury, 1950), $5.95. A classic recounting of Luther's life and struggles.

Lutheranism: A Restatement in Question and Answer Form, Martin E. Marty (Cathedral Directory, 1995), $2.25. Available through Augsburg Fortress.

Martin Luther (Vision Video), $14.99. The 1956 black and white rendition of Luther's conflict with Rome. Available through Augsburg Fortress.

The Augsburg Confession, trans. Theodore Tappert (Augsburg Fortress, 1980), $7.00. The basic, founding document of the Lutheran Reformation.

LUTHERAN–EPISCOPAL DIALOGUE

A Commentary on "Concordat of Agreement" (LED), ed. Daniel F. Martensen and James E. Griffiss (Forward Movement; Augsburg Fortress, 1994), $11.00.

Concordat of Agreement: Supporting Essays (LED), ed. Daniel F. Martensen (Forward Movement; Augsburg Fortress, 1995), $5.00.

Implications of the Gospel (LED III) (Forward Movement; Augsburg Fortress, 1988), $5.00.

What Can We Share? The LED II Report, ed. William Norgren (Forward Movement, 1985), $.50.

Who are the Episcopalians? (Augsburg Fortress, 1998), $5.00 plus shipping charges. A 17-minute video offering an overview of the Episcopal Church.

Who are the Lutherans? (Augsburg Fortress, 1998), $15.00 plus shipping. A 33-minute video offering an overview of the Evangelical Lutheran Church in America. A set of both videos may be ordered for $17.50.

The ELCA Resource Information Service (800-638-3522). Free packet of Lutheran-Episcopal educational materials containing an introduction to Called to Common Mission and ideas for joint prayer gatherings, among other materials.

AUTHORS

The Rev. Dr. G. Scott Cady. E-mail: stptr@netzero.net.

The Rev. Christopher L. Webber. E-mail: clwebber@aol.com.

Cowley Publications is a ministry of the Society of St. John the Evangelist, a religious community for men in the Episcopal Church. Emerging from the Society's tradition of prayer, theological reflection, and diversity of mission, the press is centered in the rich heritage of the Anglican Communion.

Cowley Publications seeks to provide books, audio cassettes, and other resources for the ongoing theological exploration and spiritual development of the Episcopal Church and others in the body of Christ. To this end, it is dedicated to developing a new generation of theological writers, encouraging them to produce timely, creative, and stimulating publications of excellence, and making these publications available widely, reaching both clergy and lay persons.